THE
SHEENS

By Lee Riley:

Patrick Duffy

Tom Cruise

THE SHEENS

Martin, Charlie, and Emilio Estevez

Lee Riley and David Shumacher

St. Martin's Press
New York

THE SHEENS: MARTIN, CHARLIE, AND EMILIO ESTEVEZ. Copyright © by 2M Communications Ltd., Lee Riley and David D. Shumacher. All rights reserved. Printed in the United States of America. No part of this book may be used or reproduced in any manner whatsoever without written permission except in the case of brief quotations embodied in critical articles or reviews. For information, address St. Martin's Press, 175 Fifth Avenue, New York, N.Y. 10010.

Library of Congress Cataloging-in-Publication Data

Riley, Lee.
 The Sheens : Martin, Charlie, and Emilio Estevez / Lee Riley
 and David Shumacher.
   p.   cm.
  ISBN 0-312-03427-X
   1. Motion picture actors and actresses—United States—
Biography.
  2. Sheen, Martin.   3. Sheen, Charlie.   4. Estevez, Emilio,
1962- .
  I. Shumacher, David.   II. Title.
  PN1998.2.R5   1989
  791.43′028′0922—dc20
  [B]   89-34931
                                                               CIP

Photo Research by: Amanda Rubin

First U.S. Edition
10 9 8 7 6 5 4 3 2 1

For Tamara

ACKNOWLEDGMENTS

The authors would like to express their gratitude to the many people who made this book possible:

To Lorraine Tilden and Ethlie Ann Vare, whose advice and guidance were invaluable;

To researchers Carole Glines, Gary Goldsberry, George Kreisberg, and Sandra Archer, whose assistance was immeasurable;

To Stephen King, Paul Gleason, Gene Siskel, Sy Richardson, Zooey Hall, Mark Chilingar, David Blum, Ken Rizzo, Berkley Blatz, Cara Poston, and Ann Sonnenshein, who gave freely of their time and insights;

To Madeleine Morel and Karen Moline, whose encouragement and faith are unending;

To Robert L. Deeds, for his unstinting support;

And especially to Steve and to Tamara, for their loyalty and understanding.

THE
SHEENS—

INTRODUCTION

"If you want to be an actor to become famous or important, it's the most absurd thing in the world you could do. You always have to remember that seven hundred million people in China will never know who you are . . . and will never care even if they do."

—Martin Sheen

AMERICA HAS NO ROYALTY; WE INVENT OUR ARISTOCRACY OUT of celluloid, and our dynasties are the heroes of Hollywood who successfully produce a next generation. From the Barrymores to the Fondas, our celebrities-by-birthright hold a special place in our imagination.

The Sheen family is outstanding even in this rarified genre. Martin Sheen is the ''actor's actor,'' a lion among his own colleagues. Eldest son Emilio Estevez is the youngest writer/actor/director in film history, and one of its most prolific. Charlie Sheen burst onto the screen with an impact and intensity that propelled him to overnight stardom. Not only that, Ramon and Renee Estevez have an ever-growing list of credits to their names. And a new generation has already been born, destined to grow up in the California sun and the Hollywood spotlight. . . .

1

2 ▪ THE SHEENS

What marked this family for greatness? How did a crippled kid from Dayton, Ohio, whose father barely spoke English, a kid whose education ended with high school and hasn't taken an acting class in his life, earn such a place in the Hollywood hierarchy? And what makes his children so rich in talent? Is this a genetic gift, some kind of hereditary acting bug? Or is it a richness of love and warmth and direction within the family? And where does the quiet one, Martin's wife and center—Janet Templeton Estevez—fit in?

The Estevez-Sheen clan is special, each member is unique. Martin said of his sons, ''Charlie has the Nth degree of everything that's human: great anger, great passion, great love. Emilio . . . is centered. He's always seemed to know what he wanted, and has gone after it in a concrete way.''

And Martin? ''I'm a working actor. Acting is the creative expression I have for all the other parts of me.''

All these other parts—father, lover, Catholic, activist, as he likes to define them—coalesce as one of the most respected men in his industry. This, then, is an attempt to define and integrate these qualities, and search for a glimpse of the man behind the actor . . . and the remarkable legacy he has given us.

▪ 1 ▪

Beginnings

MARTIN SHEEN'S START IN LIFE WAS HARDLY WHAT ONE WOULD consider the appropriate foundation for establishing a Hollywood acting dynasty. He had the start in life that usually leads to food stamps.

Born Ramon Estevez on August 3, 1940 to an Irish mother and a Spanish father, he was the seventh son of ten children: nine boys and a girl. His mother, a first-generation immigrant, endured twelve pregnancies from which these ten children survived. Ramon arrived small, weak, and defective; his left arm was three inches shorter than his right. "My arm was smashed with the forceps at birth, and it didn't quite develop," he explained in 1987, adding that his peers referred to him as a cripple. "It's still almost useless, but I'm glad I've got it."

The family of twelve lived in a three-bedroom house, sleeping two to a bed. They were oppressively poor, but to the future Martin Sheen, the poverty was never oppressive. "There were bigger families in our parish," he said.

"There were kids from families of fourteen children—and they were all poor." When Ramon was only eleven, his mother—so devout a Catholic that she led the family in reciting the rosary every night after dinner—died.

Mary Ann Phelan had come to this country in fear of her life, because her father and brothers were active in the Irish Republican Army. She spoke English with a heavy brogue, and loved to sing Irish folk songs for her children. She met her husband at a citizenship class for prospective Americans.

Francesco Estevez had immigrated from Vigo, Spain, but because of hard feelings over the Spanish-American War, arrived in America via Cuba. He had worked in the sugarcane fields there for several years before eventually settling in Dayton, Ohio.

"I loved my father deeply," said Sheen. "He was the best man I ever knew. . . . For him, life was a mystery to be lived, rather than a series of problems to be solved. And he really lived his life that way."

Francesco was just a little, shy man who rarely even spoke outside the home because he was so self-conscious of his Spanish accent. He paid cash for everything, had an explosive temper, and was disappointed when Martin chose an acting career over going to college. Francesco worked as a drill-press operator for the National Cash Register Company for forty-seven years, most of his life.

After his wife's death, Francesco feared that he would be unable to keep the large family together. He was advised to put some of the children into foster homes, where they would be better cared for financially. But he could not bear to break up the close-knit brood, no matter what the hardships. With the help and encouragement of the local parish, Holy Trinity, he struggled and made ends meet. Where money ran short, love filled the gap.

The church remained a major component of the children's young lives and left an indelible impression on

Ramon/Martin—who would take his very name from a church leader. After a long lapse of faith, he today considers himself a steadfast Catholic.

During Ramon's childhood, church and family were inextricably intertwined in his life. Every morning before school, he would serve as an altar boy at a traditional Latin mass. The memorization and recitation of prayers; the glow of the candlelight and smell of incense; the colorful vestments and choreographed moves . . . the setting was not so very different from an elaborate movie set. In retrospect, Martin noted, "Serving mass was really theatrical. We dressed up in costumes. It was a performance. At one point I considered the priesthood, but chose acting instead."

As a boy, Ramon *believed* in his church and his God. His older brother, Michael, liked to tell the story of the time he (Michael) was competing in a local golf tournament. Ramon stood at the sidelines, rosary in hand, and prayed for his victory. He promised God he would make a novena (a prescribed series of prayers over a period of several days) if his brother won.

Michael won; Martin prayed.

Golf was more than a hobby in the Estevez household; it was a lifeline. Out of necessity, all the boys took jobs at an early age, usually becoming junior breadwinners before they turned ten. One favored form of employment was caddying at the local country club—and it was here that young Ramon learned his first lessons in sociopolitical realities.

Martin caddied from the time he was nine until the age of eighteen. "It was there, at the country club," said Martin more than a decade later, "that I began to realize that the whole world wasn't poor. Some people had a great deal of money, as well as position and power in the community. I resented some of them—not for what they had, but for the way they used or abused it."

At the tender age of fifteen, Ramon—or Ray, as his friends called him—led his fellow caddies out on an unheard-of strike against the club because they were not being paid as much as caddies at a neighboring golf course. Staging the strike on a Tuesday was perfect timing. Many doctors and lawyers normally filled the links on Wednesdays, so the strike was brought to a speedy end in just one day.

Ramon, however, was not back on the greens that Thursday. His first public display of social activism got him summarily fired. Still, he managed to find another job at the rival country club.

Daily routine consisted of school, caddying eighteen holes, and looking for lost golf balls until dark. Evenings were spent with Francesco, who came home exhausted but never tired of spending time with his children.

School was parochial, run by the Sisters of Notre Dame. The sisters were experts at keeping their charges in line with doses of both vinegar and honey. "The nuns were strict disciplinarians. They'd beat the hell out of you and then slip you money under the table for something you really needed. They had charity and compassion," recalled Martin in 1979.

The family managed to stay together.

For pocket money, Ramon collected empty bottles to raise the fifteen-cent-admission for a Saturday movie matinee. The movies were magic, an escape, and a promise. "I was a young child living more in my imagination than in reality," Martin mused later. "When I began to go to movies I realized that's what I was, that's what I wanted to do. I knew I was an actor."

During his years at Chaminade High School, taught by the Marinist fathers, Ramon became active in the parish teen club. He was its first president, in fact, and his peers admired his ability to be serious, compassionate, and funny.

It was during the high school years that he began amateur acting work in a secular environment.

By the time Ramon was seventeen, he had progressed from staging plays without props and reciting poetry from milk crates and boasted a total of fourteen high school plays on his resumé. The capper was an appearance on a local talent show, *The Rising Generation*, that was loosely based on *The Ted Mack Amateur Hour*, where the winners were chosen by postcard votes sent in by the audience. Ramon Estevez closed out his scholastic career with a dramatic reading from the Book of Genesis and won the popularity poll. His prize: a trip to New York City and an audition at CBS television.

That trip was a turning point in Ramon Estevez's life. As he told *Rolling Stone* interviewer Jean Vallely, "My senior year was one of the best times in my life. I knew I was going to New York and spent the entire year dreaming about it. I let my hair grow long, listened to a lot of music, and was very aware of the times. There were two big influences on me, James Dean and Elvis Presley, and no one who had that kind of effect on me came along until Bob Dylan . . . my patron saint."

As it turned out, Ramon couldn't wait to fly away to the Big Apple. In fact, he admitted later, "I didn't give a damn about school. I made up my mind in senior year that I was going to be an actor . . . I never thought of myself as anything but an actor."

With some extra cash in his pocket from selling Christmas trees and a loan from the parish priest, Martin arrived in New York City on February 1, 1959—the day before Buddy Holly died in a plane crash. That day "was the start of my adult life," said Sheen. He worked as a night-shift stockboy at American Express for forty dollars a week, while running to auditions during the day.

It was during this period that Ramon Estevez changed his name. Not only did he not look particularly Hispanic, but he feared that his real Latino monicker would be a distinct handicap in an acting career. Even today, ethnic pigeonholes are hard to escape in film and television.

The name "Martin Sheen" had a dual genesis. The first half honored a man named Robert Dale Martin, the casting director at CBS who had encouraged young Ramon when he arrived for that first audition. "Sheen" was actually a tribute to Bishop Fulton J. Sheen, a greatly admired church leader at the time and a man young Estevez considered "an extraordinary actor" in his own right.

While most articles written about Martin Sheen credit the bishop for inspiring his stage name, later ones often don't mention it. Somewhere along the way, Martin's fame outreached the bishop's, and it became too difficult to explain the nomenclature. Martin told a *Sunday Woman* magazine reporter in 1979, "It's Irish and I look Irish and it's short and easy to pronounce and spell." A year later he told *Cosmopolitan* magazine, "I just liked the way it sounded." To this day, however, Ramon G. Estevez is the name on all of Martin Sheen's official documents—even his driver's license.

Bishop Sheen was only one of Martin Sheen's early idols. Along with James Cagney, Frank Sinatra, and Bob Dylan, Martin has said, "I worshipped James Dean. He was to my generation what Dylan is to the present. That brief time he was alive, he was something to reach for, a grand, noble actor.

"I loved him but, very early in my career, I also learned that to imitate the living was mockery and to imitate the dead was robbery. Do you remember that quote?" he asked the reporter he was conversing with. "It's what Johnny Cash said about Bob Dylan on the back of the record album *Nashville Skyline*."

In New York, Martin became the quintessential starving young actor. Without the funds for acting lessons, Sheen and some friends formed a group called the Actor's Co-Op under the guidance of Vasek Simek; they performed in showcase presentations in a loft near the old Madison Square Garden building. Another struggling young actor in the group was named Barbra Streisand, a "sweet kid from Brooklyn, very shy and funny," as Martin remembered her. "No one knew she could sing. And then, lo and behold, she was on Broadway as a star."

It was while Streisand starred in *Funny Girl* that Sheen was fired by American Express ("They should have fired me months earlier; I was never there!") and began work as a stagehand/prop-master for a repertory group. Julian Beck and Judith Malina's Living Theater was an avant-garde off-off-Broadway troupe, later referred to as "a prototype of some of the hippie communes of the late 1960s." It was there that Martin met another struggling-actor destined-to-be-somebody, Al Pacino.

"We worked together, cleaning toilets, sweeping, painting," remembered Martin. "We moved props for Allen Ginsberg and John Cage . . . I met Larry Rivers . . . and I got paid for acting in a play, *Purgatory* by William Butler Yeats. I got five dollars."

These were heady times. John F. Kennedy was running for President. Camelot and Bob Dylan were in the air— along with marijuana smoke, which the young adults were not above experimenting with. "I used to take that stuff," Sheen told *US* magazine in 1980, "a long time before it was even fashionable." Martin also started hanging around the Catholic Worker, a group of political activists.

It was in 1961 that Martin met Janet Templeton, a student at the New School for Social Research in New York, through a mutual actor-friend at a backstage party. The attraction, Martin told *Rolling Stone*, was not mutual at first, but he was persistent. Admitted Martin, "I was thinking about getting laid . . . Janet was my first." Janet yielded to his attentions, beginning what would prove to be a lifelong love.

Soon the couple began living together—a move that got them evicted from Janet's apartment because cohabitation was considered sinful by her landlord. They lived on love, hope, and macaroni casseroles as Martin waited for his break in the impossible industry he had chosen.

The money for acting school never did materialize, and to this day, Martin Sheen does not boast any formal acting school training. But his natural abilities were enough to get him chosen to replace Gary Goodrow in the role of Ernie in *The Connection*, a play that took a bold look at drug addiction and awed and shocked theatergoers with its frank dialogue.

Matt Clark, then the stage manager of *The Connection* and still a friend of the Sheen family, later recalled, "Marty was funny. He was the only serious actor I ever knew who didn't care to study. He used to say that study was just reassurance. He didn't have to be reassured."

That same year, 1961, Janet quit school and the couple went to London on tour with the play.

▪ 2 ▪

Two Can Live as Cheaply . . .

ONCE BACK IN AMERICA, MARTIN AND JANET MARRIED ON December 23, 1961, adding a new flavor to the family melting pot: Janet is part Jewish, among other ethnic varieties. While Martin juggled casting calls with odd jobs (usher in a Manhattan theater, soda jerk in the Bronx, car washer, busboy), Janet settled into their meager nest. While they never dreamed at the time that they would leave New York City for the milder climes of Malibu, Janet recalled that "we kept moving all the time—to a cheaper apartment."

Martin quipped in 1980, "Thursday was garbage day, and Wednesday night we'd go out . . . and collect. We decorated three or four apartments from the street. On the day we were married, I put on a big army coat with pockets inside and out, and I went to the supermarket to steal bologna and cheese." The lack of money often led to stress and spats; unskilled "day jobs" and pitiful bank accounts took their toll. Once, Martin recalled, the couple was having a not-unusual fight about money: "She said,

11

'I'll show you,' went to her purse, and tore up seventy dollars. I spent hours taping that money back together!''

Their first child, Emilio, was born early in 1962. And it was while the couple was living on Staten Island that second son Ramon came into the world—without medical assistance. ''I delivered one of my children myself,'' Sheen recalled. ''That's the kind of financial shape I was in. It was the most stupid thing I could have done. I almost lost my wife and my baby.'' To this day, Sheen does as much as he can to make sure that people do not have to exist in this country without access to a doctor's care.

By 1963, Martin was beginning to make some headway in his career. He played an alcoholic wife-beater in a segment of the television series *East Side, West Side*, starring George C. Scott. ''Martin did a fine job for me,'' Scott recalled for *After Dark* magazine almost a decade later. ''I remember he had a wonderful sweetness about him as a person and was such a calm, gentlemanly-type fellow—and when he played the part he was absolutely wild and crazy and tore the whole joint up and everything. I was very impressed with his work. And certainly impressed with him as a human being.''

In 1964, Sheen made his Broadway debut in *Never Live Over a Pretzel Factory*; later that same year he received public and critical acclaim with Jack Albertson and Irene Dailey in Frank Gilroy's Pulitzer Prize-winning play, *The Subject Was Roses*. He and Albertson were both nominated for Tony Awards; Albertson won. But the victor later noted, ''I beat out Marty only because mine was the stronger part.''

This was not only the first but just about the last acting award Martin would ever vie for—not because his work wasn't considered deserving, but because he consistently withdrew his name from competition. He simply disagrees with the concept of singling out individual players for approval over and above their fellows. Back then, though, as he later told *Variety*, "I didn't bother with it. I knew it wouldn't make any difference if I had. I just let it pass, and it did."

During the run of *The Subject Was Roses*, Sheen suggested that the general manager of the theater organize a benefit performance to raise funds for the growing civil-rights movement. He also initiated the involvement of old friend Barbra Streisand and of Sammy Davis, Jr., who was then appearing in *Golden Boy*. Most of Broadway was contributing its support for racial equality that night, as receipts from various box offices were funneled into human-rights coffers. Sheen remembered that another famous Martin—Reverend Martin Luther King, Jr.—was backstage at the theater that night, but in the confusion he never got to shake hands with another one of his many heroes.

By now it was obvious that Sheen as an actor had to expand his venues if he was going to support a wife and two sons—soon to be three sons, as Carlos (now Charlie) was due in 1965. It was time to get into the lucrative, if not particularly challenging, field of serial television. Sheen attacked TV with a vengeance: his episodic television resumé included roles on *The Defenders, Route 66, Medical Center, The Mod Squad, The F.B.I.* and even *My Three Sons*. For much of 1967, he was a regular on the daytime soap opera *As the World Turns*, playing the part of Jack Davis.

Actor Zooey Hall, who today has a recurring role on the daytime drama *The Young and the Restless*, guest-starred with Sheen in an early episode of *The F.B.I.* "We were both playing members of a Mafia family trying to make our marks," he recalled. "Martin's character was sent to kill someone on behalf of his godfather within the family, but had gotten himself involved with a character played by Meg Foster. He didn't make the hit he was contracted to do, so I was sent to kill him and Foster's character. We had a big chase sequence on the docks. At one point, he trips and falls and I have the opportunity to kill him.

"What I remember most about Sheen is how he'd be standing by, watching as my close-ups were being shot. The camera was shooting up from the ground, as if it were his point of view. He was standing by, watching this very intently. Afterwards, he came up and complimented me on the simplicity and honesty of my work. I had the feeling he was really studying my technique in front of the camera. I may be just guessing now, but I think he had then done some work in episodic television, but was still getting familiar with camera technique. If you were in one Quinn Martin show and he liked your work, chances are you'd get a role in other Quinn Martin series. When Sheen and I worked together, he had more experience working onstage.

"I remember that some of his children—two or three of them—were on the set with him that day," continued Hall. "My impression of him was that he was a serious and hardworking actor and a caring father."

Martin continued to appear on the boards throughout this period. He worked with producer Joseph Papp in *Romeo and Juliet* and did a controversial, mod production of *Hamlet*. In this unusual vision of Shakespeare, Sheen played the mournful Dane as a Puerto Rican janitor. The play was a flop, but critics noted, "The part is played by a gifted young actor, Martin Sheen, who is so mercurial and nimble (physically and verbally) and handles his brainless assignments with such poise that it may be entirely because of him that the proceedings are not a bore."

Martin's association with Papp continues today, with ongoing plans for a New York showcase as well as Sheen's continued encouragement of his son Charlie toward the legitimate theater.

In 1967, Sheen landed his first feature-film role in *The Incident*, with Tony Musante. The pair played drunken hoodlums who terrorize subway passengers in the bowels of Manhattan. It was in that same year that Martin was

strongly attracted to a daring new stage play in prepro-
duction. "I read three pages of this new musical and I
knew it would be great," he told *Woman's Wear Daily*
(WWD). (As it happened, he didn't get a part in the New
York "tribe" of *Hair*.)

A film veteran at last, Martin was ready to conquer
Hollywood. His first Los Angeles-based role was in an
episode of *Outer Limits* and by the late sixties, he was
traveling from New York to L.A. on a regular basis. The
first trip, however, was the most memorable—and not
only because it was the first. It turned out that the bus he
was riding on broke down outside of Albuquerque, New
Mexico; Martin and five other passengers literally pushed
the bus down the highway until it jump-started.

Soon the parts began to roll in: He did the screen
version of *The Subject Was Roses*, and played the small
role of Lieutenant Dobbs in the film adaptation of Joseph
Heller'a anti-war novel, *Catch-22*. Colleagues from that
film's Mexican location setting remembered Martin Sheen
well. This was the guy who refused to stay with everyone
else in Guaymas at the plush Playa de Cortes Hotel. When
they saw the conditions under which the locals lived,
Martin and Janet chose instead to live among the native
villagers, many of whom subsisted near starvation. The
Sheens became a one-family Peace Corps, giving away
most of their clothing, food, and kitchen and bathroom
supplics.

It was also during that Guaymas location shoot that the
Sheens fell in love with warm weather, and made the
decision to relocate the Estevez clan to Malibu, California.
In California, said Martin, "You can dress any way, act
any way, start a religion—no one will put you down."

It wasn't very long after the move west in 1969 that
George C. Scott beckoned Martin back to the New York
stage. Scott was producing the off-Broadway version of
South African playwright Athol Fugard's *Hello and Good-*

bye, about the emotional confrontation of a son and daughter in the family of an Afrikaaner railwayman after years of separation. Colleen Dewhurst played the embittered prostitute sister; Sheen replaced another actor as the hysterical brother. The play ran only forty-five performances, but helped cement the Scott-Sheen friendship.

Back in Los Angeles, a new art form called the "MoW" —Movie of the Week—was in full gear, allowing the small screen to tackle productions and subjects that would be impossible on the expensive silver-screen scale. Some telemovies were simply churned out, but others were landmarks in home entertainment. Martin appeared in *Then Came Bronson*; *Goodbye, Raggedy Ann*; *Mongo's Back in Town*; *Welcome Home, Johnny Bristol*. And then, on November 1, 1972, he starred in one of the landmark TV movies of its day, *That Certain Summer*, alongside Hal Holbrook. It was television's first serious, sympathetic portrayal of homosexuality, with Sheen and Holbrook playing the lovers.

That Certain Summer was among the most honored productions of 1972, and Martin Sheen was nominated for an Emmy Award for his sensitive portrayal. He turned it down.

In a letter to the Academy of Television Arts and Sciences, Sheen wrote, "I appreciate the honor, but on personal principles I would like my name to be taken off the ballot. I don't feel that actors should compete against each other." The name Martin Sheen was stricken from the annals of Emmy history, and the supporting actor with the next highest number of votes in the category—James Brolin of the *Marcus Welby, MD* series—was put on the ballot instead.

▪ 3 ▪

Badlands, Good Times

IN 1958, A NINETEEN-YEAR-OLD BOY NAMED CHARLES STARK-
weather took his fourteen-year-old girlfriend, Caril Fugate, on a murder spree through Lincoln, Nebraska. By the
time they were caught they had killed ten people, including Fugate's mother, stepfather, and half-sister. In separate
trials, both Starkweather and Fugate were convicted of
murder. He was executed in the electric chair; she was
sentenced to life imprisonment.

Badlands was director Terrence Malick's vision of the
Starkweather case. The names, places, and the manner of
dying had been changed: Martin Sheen was a South Da-
kota garbage collector named Kit Caruthers; Sissy Spacek
was the girl sociopath, Holly. The 1972 movie was pre-
dicted to make Martin Sheen a major star.

"I was terribly excited after reading the script," Sheen
told a *WWD* reporter, looking back on a movie he still
feels is one of his best. Of his character, he recalled:
"Even his capture would be on his own terms. He combed

17

his hair, took his pulse, and built a monument to himself. He saw his capture as an historical event. Even when he killed, it was on an existential level. There was no vengeance or thrill motive. His gun was his magic wand. He used it the same way the C.I.A. uses its weapons to overthrow governments and the U.S. uses bombs. We're all taught from the time we're children to use things to remove obstacles.''

Sheen's friend and admirer George C. Scott was bowled over by Martin's work in *Badlands*. Scott commented, ''He can play a totally amoral character and still come off sympathetically. I am stunned. Stunned. He is one of the best young actors alive.''

Today, Martin will not play a role as violent as the mass murderer. But at the time, he felt there were justifications for this type of characterization—and those justifications did not have dollar signs on them. ''There are many more reasons for doing a role than just the money,'' Martin told a television interviewer. ''I look at it in my own life this way: that the part can offer me an opportunity to examine a part of myself that ordinarily I might not do. It might help me get to an area of myself that I might not ordinarily be able to get to. It's like being given a license that says, 'All right now, you can examine this.' And no one is the wiser because the craft is the art or the profession.''

Playing a psychotic killer like Caruthers allowed Sheen ''to explore the possibility that I had those tendencies in me as well. I didn't ignore or deny them; I explored them. I disapprove of killing, I disapprove of harming people, but I get angry and hurt people. That's violence. If I were to deny that, it would be dangerous. A lot of people say, 'Well, I'm a nonviolent person,' yet they contribute to organizations that buy and sell weapons. Or they believe in keeping some segments of our society down. We engage in all sorts of activity for our own benefit that is to the detriment of other people. That's very violent.''

New York Times critic Vincent Canby noted in his review of *Badlands*: "Kit and Holly are out of touch with their feelings, and it's the scary suggestion of *Badlands* that this isn't an especially abnormal condition in this time and place. Although they talk, they cannot communicate, within themselves or to each other. The language they use is made up of phrases learned by rote. . . . Miss Spacek manages the rather grand feat of being simultaneously transparent and mysterious, sweet and heedlessly cruel. Sheen, who does look a lot like James Dean, whom Kit fancies, has what may be the role of his career."

Martin was obsessive about the "role of his career." There was one scene set in a gas station, and Martin made a point of personally picking up all the flip-top can rings from the filming area, because in 1959 soda cans didn't have the easy-open tabs. "We had to be careful all along," detail-attentive Sheen told the *WWD* reporter. "You can never wing it. Acting is not an accident. I'm appalled to see inexperienced actors hired because of their looks or personality and young players made overnight successes when they don't know what they're doing."

Ironically, the role of Kit Caruthers almost went to the young actor who "assassinated" Martin back in *The F.B.I.*: Zooey Hall. Hall had then been receiving kudos for his intense work in the prison movie *Fortune and Men's Eyes.* Recalled Hall, "Terry Malick contacted me because he was considering me for the lead in *Badlands*. I had just gotten back from working on another movie in Europe, and Terry called me at home. He said he was pretty much decided on me for the lead in this film and wanted me to come up to his house to shoot some footage. The project sounded very interesting to me, so I agreed. At his place I met an actress, Sissy Spacek, whom I had never heard of before. Terry filmed the two of us. The next thing I heard was that Martin Sheen had gotten the part. He did a fine job of it."

Despite the excellence of *Badlands*, its depressing subject matter made it basically unacceptable commercially. While it received praise from the critics, the movie was simply seen by too few people to propel Martin to the universal acclaim those who did see it felt he deserved.

In 1972, Sheen and his family shared a small and crowded rented house in Tucson, Arizona for six weeks while Martin worked on the movie *Rage*. The project reunited Sheen with George C. Scott, who starred in and directed the feature film that ended up becoming one of that great actor's (another who refuses actors' awards) least liked.

It's the story of a father's vengeance for his son's death, a death brought about by an accident in a secret chemical warfare experiment. Scott tries to blow open the military's attempt at a cover-up, and Sheen was all but unnoticed in his role as an Army physician. But for Sheen, the reward was working alongside Scott. Martin said that sharing scenes with George was like "being in a ring with a heavyweight. And I'm about bantam weight by comparison."

For his next role, a 1973 adaptation of Brian Moore's novella *Catholics*, Martin was able to go back to his altar-boy days and don the priest's robes as Father Kinsella. He played a reformer sent to sway a group of Latin ritists who had holed up in an abbey off the coast of Ireland. Although the CBS *Playhouse 90* piece was considered "another impressive step towards superstardom" for Martin, what he has best remembered about the production was that he bought a Super-8 camera for his little boys— Emilio, Ramon, and Carlos. It was supposed to be something to keep them occupied while he worked; little did he know that it would spark the interest of a new generation of entertainment-industry dynamos.

In March of 1974 came another heralded TV movie, the two-and-a-half-hour special, *The Execution of Private Slovik*. Martin played the title character in yet another downer drama—the saga of the only American soldier since the

Civil War to be shot for desertion. He took the part so seriously, remembered his wife, that "he was absolutely impossible during that period. He couldn't stop being Slovik, even at home."

In real life, Sheen was never in the military. "I married young, and nothing much was happening at the time, but I probably would have gone if called," he has said. "I'd probably have been one of the guys in the firing squad.

"The Slovik case is relevant today because human life is sacred. If we're responsible for it, we have to take it seriously."

It's not only life that Martin Sheen takes seriously. He also takes acting very, very seriously. When *Private Slovik* was released he told *TV Guide*, "People think acting is an accident. It's not. It's calculated, planned, scrutinized, rehearsed. A performer has to know what he's doing every instant, to invent and improvise and feel, to bleed a little or else there's no growth . . . God, how I love to act!"

It was also in 1974 that Martin made *Pretty Boy Floyd,* a movie made memorable because it gave him the chance to bring yet another member of his family into the business: his brother, Joseph Estevez. Joe, who worked at a Frigidaire factory in Ohio at the time, had been acting in local amateur theater groups. He auditioned for and won the role of "E.W." in the television movie. The experience spurred a major change in Joseph's life; today, working under the name of Joe Phelan (his mother's maiden name), he is a professional actor himself.

If Joseph was becoming enamored of the actor's calling, his brother was becoming disenchanted with it at times. In August of 1975, Martin took the opportunity at a luncheon in his honor (for his work with James Farentino in *Death of a Salesman*) to express his displeasure with acting awards and the quality of prime-time television: "To engage in a campaign to receive a prize is juvenile. Why should actors be made to compete against each other?" he asked.

He continued by describing network fare as "the garbage that starts in the morning and continues all day . . . it's on a sixth-grade level." He also contended that programmers "assume that this is a nation of idiots. You just have to watch the tube every night to see what I'm talking about. To improve TV, you have to start over and assume that people are intelligent. Some of the people running the programs may not be as intelligent as the audiences are."

There are reasons for the relative lack of quality on television. "They work too fast on TV, they're too heavily censored, and the scripts are weak," declared Sheen. "Besides, you have to compete with actual events shown on newscasts. Nothing I've done on television can compare with seeing one real man get killed."

Still, Martin continued to work in the television medium, and gradually began to develop a certain respect for it. His hotheadedness cooled. Several years after those 1975 comments, he conceded, "Some people in show business are still snobbish towards TV. They're nuts. If TV acting is good enough for George C. Scott and Laurence Olivier, who are they to say?" A decade after his luncheon outburst, Martin had come full circle. "I work very often for the money. I have no altruistic set of values I apply to my work," he said. "I find it very difficult to turn down money for doing something I don't believe in. I'm not strong enough to say no."

We all have to grow up sometime. And Martin Sheen is only human.

▪ 4 ▪

Apocalypse Now

MARTIN SHEEN WAS NOT THE FIRST ACTOR OF CHOICE FOR THE role of Captain Ben Willard in Francis Ford Coppola's *Apocalypse Now*. Steve McQueen had been asked originally, but wanted $3 million to do the project. Al Pacino turned it down. Jack Nicholson was interested but was working on another film. Eventually, Coppola hired Harvey Keitel (*Mean Streets, Taxi Driver*), but Keitel walked off the set in a contract dispute after three weeks.

It turned out that Sheen, just back from filming *The Cassandra Crossing* in Rome, ran into Coppola at the airport; the director was himself en route from the Philippines. Martin had been one of the early people considered—and rejected—for the part. This time, however, the timing was right. On April 27, 1976, Martin Sheen began a sixteen-month "journey into darkness" that would change his life.

The role was a challenge. Ben Willard is young, cynical, and war-weary; he's also a killer-for-hire. Willard has

23

been assigned to find and "terminate with extreme preju-
dice" the renegade and psychotic Colonel Kurtz, played
by Marlon Brando, in his Cambodian jungle retreat. A
Vietnam war story based on Joseph Conrad's *Heart of
Darkness, Apocalypse Now* was, as Sheen put it, certain to
be "one of the most talked-about films in motion-picture
history." For many reasons, it was.

For one thing, it was one of the most logistically horren-
dous shoots in motion-picture history. Eight weeks into
filming, typhoon Olga brought production to a halt. On
May 16, 1976, a six-day rainstorm began that brought
more than forty inches of rain to the location and destroyed
many of the film's standing sets. The town of Luzon was
all but demolished. There was a two-month hiatus while
the technical crew salvaged what they could from the
destruction and rebuilt the rest.

It was when the film resumed production that Martin
Sheen made one of the most memorable opening scenes
ever filmed. These few moments established so much
character—and with such economy, grace, and intensity—
that Sheen effortlessly embodied, for posterity, all his
ideas about acting. Five years before laying down this
remarkable bit of footage, he had said, "When I walk in
front of a camera I ask myself, 'Why are you so scared?
What are you hiding?' Then I begin to feel the reality of
the situation. I can't admit to the fear of what the camera
does . . . it catches you. As actors we do things in public
that ordinary people do alone. We must do it publicly. . . .
Some of our greatest actors have difficulty stripping themselves. It takes enormous courage to let it—the rage, the
fear, the hurt—come out."

In that famous opening scene of *Apocalypse Now*, Martin Sheen (Captain Willard) is literally naked in a Saigon
hotel room. As "This Is the End" by the Doors plays on
the soundtrack, he moves around the room practicing martial-
arts moves and then catches his reflection in the mirror. He

studies himself more closely in the glass and becomes so enraged and so repulsed by the person he sees that he punches the mirror to destroy the image. The mirror breaks; his hand bleeds. Willard smears his blood over his face and body.

"The director decided what was necessary in the beginning of the film was to show a guy who was suicidal, drunk, unhappy," explained Sheen. "He was no ordinary hero. He was a professional killer, which is what a soldier is. This soldier had to deal with death to the utmost degree. He had to kill his own people. He was unhappy, and very confused."

When he did that scene, Martin admitted, "I was intoxicated. I had been drinking all day. I'd lived in that room for a couple of days, day and night. I had no business being on the screen. Francis didn't want me to do it, but I insisted. . . . He was very compassionate, very sweet . . . I was a raving lunatic."

Coppola's wife, Eleanor, wrote in her book *Notes*, about the *Apocalypse* experience, that when Martin's hand started to bleed, "Francis said his impulse was to cut the scene and call the nurse, but Marty was doing the scene. He had gotten to the place where some part of him and Willard merged. Francis had a moment of not wanting to be a vampire, sucking Marty's blood for the camera, and not wanting to turn off the camera when Marty was Willard. He left it running."

As the cameras rolled, Martin collapsed on the bed, holding hands with Coppola and others around him as he sang "Amazing Grace" and bled through the wrappings someone in the crew had put on his hand. Janet and Emilio were called, but it was two hours before they were able to get Martin back to the hotel.

"That scene wasn't in the script," Sheen has since confessed on numerous occasions. "It was me. At least, it was me at the time. That was something I invented that came out of the dark side of me . . . . I was a very confused man. We shot it on August third, nineteen seventy-six—my thirty-sixth birthday. I'll never forget that day for as long as I live.

"I wrestled with the devil on-camera, with a spirit inside me that I detested. Wrestled with it, brought it out in the open—and saw that devil and saw myself. A pain was escaping from me. A pain that just jumped out of my throat. It left me wandering and dazed for a while, but it was just one of those demons that I had not exorcised until then."

Martin refused to look at the rushes of that landmark scene, much as Coppola wanted him to see what amazing work he had done. In fact, the first time Martin Sheen saw himself capturing the screen at the opening of *Apocalypse Now* was in a movie theater. Said Sheen later, "It's part of myself I'm not able to look at; I'm not able to deal with it."

Martin had a premonition that he would not get out of the Philippines in one piece. At one point, he even came back to Los Angeles for several weeks, after a falling-out with his director. When the quarrel was patched up, Sheen returned to Manila filled with an unnamed dread. "I was afraid that I wouldn't come out of there alive, through an accident or something else that would happen to me," he told friends at the time and later admitted to the press.

"Working on that movie was the roughest thing I ever did in my life, both physically and emotionally," Sheen told a *Family Weekly* reporter. "I always had some illness or another, and until the last six weeks of shooting, we never knew when we were going to finish the film."

And then it happened: Late one night he was in his cabin in the mountains when he was awakened by a burning pain in his chest. By morning the pain had increased, and Martin felt dizzy and faint. He almost passed out. Rolling onto the floor, he dressed himself, then crawled on his hands and knees down a dirt path to the road where a guard gathered him up and carried him to the set. From there, a helicopter flew him through heavy winds to Manila.

It was March 5, 1977. "I was having a heart attack, and I ended up in the hospital," Martin said simply. "But the experience changed my life."

Five years earlier, when *Apocalypse Now* was no more than a handful of notes on Francis Ford Coppola's desk, Martin had expressed the desire to retreat within himself, to retire perhaps to a damp forest in Spain and sit thoughtfully in a cold stone house. He envisioned, in many ways, the isolated environment that a heart attack ended up creating for him: "I want to see if I can listen to the silence. To be quiet. For meditation. To listen to my children. I really want to see how much excess baggage I've acquired in my life. With my life. How many crosses I've got. I want to see if I can drop a few of these. . . . I want to take a look at myself . . . see where I am with me. I want to tear down, rebuild a little, remodel. I want to expose myself to change. I expect I'll be a different person if I can do it," he said at the time.

Five years later, the "remodeling" still hadn't been done. And Martin Sheen imploded.

"I was fragmented emotionally, physically, and spiritually . . . I was almost nonexistent, not in touch with my spirit at all. I was not in command of my own life," said Martin. "After the heart attack, as I lay in the hospital, I said to myself, 'You're sick because you're not taking care of yourself. This is a warning. I resolved to take better care of myself, and I prayed."

Martin was close to death. He asked for a priest to administer the last rites even though, at the time, he was a "fallen-away" Catholic who "didn't believe in God, but does believe Mary was His mother." During his three weeks in the hospital and three weeks of recuperation, Janet was at his side—sometimes even sleeping on the floor of the intensive-care unit at the Manila hospital. She arranged for a New York-based psychiatrist to counsel Sheen in long-distance telephone therapy. Meanwhile, production-company press releases referred to his heart attack and emotional collapse as "heat exhaustion."

To Martin, his heart attack was the manifestation of a spiritual, not simply a physical, illness. It was recompense for a life improperly lived. "I was the only one I knew or cared about," he confessed to *Elle* magazine many years later. "I wanted to be a movie star, to be known, to be loved. Here I was in the middle of 'my big chance' and I nearly lost it. My spirit sent me a clear message: 'You are going to have to change,' it said. 'I cannot live in you. I'm outta here.' And I said, 'Hold on! I'll make some changes.' "

From March 5 through April 19, until Martin was well enough to return to work, filming on *Apocalypse* continued. Martin's brother Joseph was flown in to act as his stand-in and double, and they shot around Willard's character entirely, whenever possible. Meanwhile, Martin was healing. He gave up cigarettes (which he had previously smoked at the rate of three to four packs a day) and he began to exercise. He stuck to a healthy diet. And, most of all, he began soul-searching, trying to find the root of what he perceived as his psychic ills.

"The experience helped me to really see my family and really appreciate who they are. They became my first priority . . . up until that point, only my career was important to me. But our careers are a projection of our egos, really. We're not our careers any more than we are our hair, clothes, or whatever. Who we really are is something far more substantial than an image. So my career was relegated to its proper place, and as a result, I have a lot more fun with it," he told *The Saturday Evening Post*.

Apocalypse Now was a blockbuster when it was released. It was nominated for Oscars in the categories of

Best Picture, Best Director, Best Editing, Best Screenplay (adapted from another medium), Best Art Direction, and Best Supporting Actor (Robert Duvall). It won for Best Cinematography and Best Sound. Once again, Martin Sheen stood by his principles and withdrew his name from the Motion Picture Academy list of nominees for the Best Actor award.

• 5 •

After the Deluge

MARTIN SHEEN SWORE AFTER HIS SOUL-DESTROYING TURN AS
Captain Ben Willard that he would never again take on a role
that was emotionally unhealthy, even though his greatest
work had been playing such characters. "There is a great
presence of violence and evil in the world," he told a
reporter. "You can't deny that. I have, because of my
experience in *Apocalypse Now*, resolved that part of myself. I'm not interested in any violent pictures. I will not
participate in them. I will not give myself because I've
been through it. I won't engage in that anymore."

But even though he wouldn't play characters troubled by
dark demons, he would still feel his own in real life for
almost four years after *Apocalypse* was finished. They
were, Sheen said, four "very, very difficult, unhappy
years."

"I didn't like myself very much. I was a very miserable
man, and I was miserable to be around. My family couldn't
live with me, and I don't blame them," he told Duo

Syndication Ltd. For three months, he separated from Janet and the children, voluntarily and unhappily. He was depressed to the point of despair.

"It was the craziest I ever felt," Martin told *Vanity Fair* reporter Stephen Schiff in 1987. "I was really bizarre . . . I was angry. I was ungrounded. I was at sea; I was really adrift . . . I would stop perfect strangers on the street and ask them if they believed in God. It was bizarre behavior." And he got into trouble as a result of it.

"One night, in San Francisco, I tied one on and decided to take this restaurant apart and I wound up in jail," Sheen told *Washington Post* reporter Tom Zito. He was separated from Janet at the time, had gone on a drinking binge—as he confessed to a *Cosmopolitan* magazine interviewer— and noticed that his wallet, with several thousand dollars in it, had been lifted. When the police showed up, he took a swing at an officer. That's how he landed in the slammer.

It was, recalled Martin, quite an eye-opening experience. "I'm sitting there with this black woman, who's still trying to get me to take some aspirin and apple juice for my hangover, thinking I'm really in big trouble now, and I ask her what she's in for. And she says, 'I shot my fella.' Just like that."

He called Janet, and when he confessed about the money, "She was just terrific. She said, 'Forget about the money. The important thing is how you're feeling, if you're all right.' I took a vow not to touch the stuff [alcohol] again. We really love each other. That's what matters."

The couple reconciled. As Sheen told reporter Rena LeBlanc, "She is the best person to ever come into my life and we have never agreed on a thing, never once, and we probably never will. And, for that reason, we always have a lot to say and fight about."

In spite of his emotional turmoil and bizarre behavior, Sheen was disciplined enough to continue to work through that 1977–81 period. He got a chance to return to his hometown of Dayton, Ohio during the filming of the TV docudrama *Blind Ambition*, and even drove by the National Cash Register building where his father and all his brothers had worked at one time or another. As he told a reporter from the *Post*, "I used to think that building was so big! They used to show movies there for the kids of the employees, and they'd have a Christmas party every year. Once they gave us each a silver dollar and I kept that big, beautiful dollar for years and years. I used to think that company was so wonderful." Now, Sheen calls his father's employers "bastards", attacking their labor practices.

With the *Post* reporter, who had landed the plum assignment of hanging out with this guy and shooting the breeze for several days, Sheen drove around in a rented Hornet and took in the local ambiance. The pair stopped off at a fast-food restaurant, and Sheen was appalled at the $2.90 per hour that the countergirl was making. She didn't seem to think the wages were so bad; in fact, she offered Martin an employment application! During breaks in filming, Sheen also stopped off at a local drama workshop. There, at least, the kids had no trouble recognizing the homegrown star.

As the disgraced presidential advisor John Dean in the Watergate saga, *Blind Ambition*, Martin found himself playing a character who, if not necessarily a goody two-shoes, was at least a nonviolent soul. His portrayal earned him the nomination for a Best Actor Golden Globe award by the Hollywood Foreign Press Association. Martin's response was typical, a telegram that read: "Many thanks for your kind consideration. I am grateful. Despite the flattery, however, I must respectfully withdraw my name as competition only serves to divide us. I pray you will hold me excused."

In 1980, Sheen made *The Final Countdown*, costarring with Katharine Ross. She described him at the time as "sort of a pixie. The parts he's played have always been very serious, but he's not like that at all. He's always joking. He's a lot of fun to be around.''

On the set, he developed a reputation as a backslapper and prankster, who would unexpectedly break into James Cagney and Humphrey Bogart impressions or a few bars of the Village People's disco hit ''In the Navy''—a song filled with gay double entendres that drove the sailor extras crazy. It's all just one more facet of a man who calls himself introspective, who says of himself, ''I'm more inclined to wonder what life is all about instead of just enjoying it.''

Actually, Martin's sense of humor is one of the first things people notice about him. And it usually surprises them. His reputation is so studiously somber and his choice of roles so weighty that he just doesn't seem like the kind of man who's going to be smiling when you meet him.

His next role was not likely to change that mistaken impression.

∎ 6 ∎

Caste and Crew:
India and Elsewhere

THE NEXT LANDMARK MOVIE ON SHEEN'S LENGTHY LIST OF credits was *Gandhi*, which had a profound effect on the deepest core of the man within the actor—not only because of the meaningful nature of the subject, but also as a result of his personal experiences during the filming of the project. *Gandhi* was Sir Richard Attenborough's long-dreamed-of biography of a young lawyer's transformation into one of the world's greatest men of peace. The beloved spiritual and political leader of India, Mohandas K. Gandhi, became a powerful twentieth century figure. Attenborough has claimed that when he read Gandhi's biography it totally changed his life. It took him twenty years to begin production on the film, but on November 26, 1980, he watched a Hindu priest bless the camera in a traditional Indian start-of-production ceremony.

In *Gandhi*, Martin played the part of Walker, a composite of several western journalists (notably Louis Fischer, Vincent Sheean, and William Shirer) who followed Gandhi's career during numerous visits to India. Each advocated Gandhi's philosophies long before he was accepted by the world at large. Producer-director Attenborough—who was knighted in 1979 for his contribution to the British stage and cinema—picked Martin for the role because, in his opinion, "Sheen is the most exciting actor to emerge from the United States during the past five years."

Martin Sheen was transfixed and transformed by India. "In India," he said, "every sense is assaulted and battered—literally—and the spirit, too." And the Sheen who emerged from working on this film was a great deal more spiritually connected than the man who first arrived on Attenborough's set. Also, he emerged much more connected with his eldest son, and it was Emilio—on location as Martin's stand-in—who was in many ways the conduit to Martin's spiritual rebirth.

"While in India, Emilio helped me in a unique way," Sheen recalled in a *Washington Post* interview. "He dove into crowds. I was afraid of the crowds, but he dove in, and I followed. . . . I saw that we are all one, all from the same father. I am in and of this, this is the mystical body of Christ."

Sheen also found the poverty in India frightening. "Particularly the suffering of the children. I was terrified. You'd see children with lice in their hair, skin already shot—they looked like old people. Their teeth were rotten . . . they had no undergarments. They were filthy all over. They grab hold of your legs, you know, until a crowd gathers. . . . After a while you really have to surrender. And I started doing that, because I started to see in the faces of these children, which I was trying to avoid, my own children. I realized, they are mine. We are all, every one of us, connected."

Unequal distribution of wealth and the oppression of the underclasses has always affected Martin strongly, even in America where the division is subtle compared to many

other parts of the world. Imagine his reaction to the juxta-
position of such great wealth and such terrible poverty.
Emilio, too, was repulsed by the chasm between the haves
and the have-nots. Once, there was a party for the cast and
crew, and Martin recalled: "The servants were treated so
badly that Emilio was disgusted. Emilio called me into the
toilet and said, 'We've got to get out of here.' I said, 'Is it
the way they're treating the help?' He said, 'Yes, they
don't even see them.' I said, 'Emilio, you must understand, they cannot see the help. If they see the help, they
see themselves.' "

Another incident that stuck out in Martin's mind was
one he related to a reporter from *Elle* magazine. Martin
and some of the other members of the film company were
granted permission to visit with Mother Teresa. He was
excited and rushed back to the hotel to tell Emilio the
news. Sheen clamored and stammered about the plans to
take an overnight train and celebrate early morning mass
with the selfless nun, who had been awarded the Nobel
Peace Prize for her devotion to the poor.

"Emilio stared at me, half smiling, and asked, 'Why?'
And I screamed back, 'Are you joking me? Didn't you
read the books I gave you about her?' 'Yes, I read them.
But why?' he repeated. 'How can you ask that?' I shrieked,
swearing I was talking to an idiot. Then Emilio, by now
laughing at my frenzy, yelled back, 'But why do you want
to meet her?' And I hurled back reflexively, 'So I can tell
everyone I met her!' Then he smiled and looked back at
me.

"I never went. I really had no business going there
anyway. I would have fainted from the poverty and been
one more obstacle for her to deal with. My son taught me
that."

Although he was raised a devout Roman Catholic, Sheen
had gradually fallen away from practicing his faith. The
separation came mainly in his late twenties, when he was

more concerned with the injustices of the world around him. "I didn't feel comfortable with Catholicism in the sixties," he said. "The church didn't take a stand in politics . . . it just wasn't active, wasn't realistic. The church wasn't strong enough to hold on to me."

But the soul-searching that occurred after his heart attack, compounded by what he saw in India, reaffirmed his childhood faith. "I came back from India shaken. Very deeply shaken. And started searching. Asking. Trying to make touch. I became a practicing Catholic once again."

Spirituality is infused in Martin Sheen's life. He has meshed his inherited Roman Catholic beliefs with personal experiences that allow him a belief in reincarnation, one that had developed long before his film work in India. Besides, as he pointed out several times, "Until the third or fourth century, the Church believed in it. I find it hard to believe I'm not Adam. We're still in the Garden of Eden. We're still trying to get back to God."

Martin believes that his work as an actor has a spiritual basis, too, and that perspective has made it easier to accept his children's career choices. "At first, the idea of them following in my career path bothered me," he said. "I thought of my own experiences. But then I rejoiced. They would find this spiritual life. That's how we find God in ourselves. Creativity is really a manifestation of the spirit, of God's presence in us. And everyone must be creative. Hopefully, we can do that through our work. But we must be creative. It's a conduit to the spirit."

The budget for the epic film *Gandhi* was $22 million. Martin's salary was a $100,000 donation from the filmmakers to a charity called Concern, which aids refugees in Third World countries. Similarly, he worked without pay and gave his $5,000 salary back to the producers of the film *In the King of Prussia*, which told the story of the Ploughshare peace movement.

It was during that project that he met Father Daniel

Berrigan, a Jesuit priest who is an activist for the peace movement in America. And it was just prior to the beginning of that filming that Martin lost his brother Michael to a heart attack (he had also lost his mother and another brother to heart attacks). Father Berrigan consoled Martin over his loss, and became his spiritual advisor and teacher.

Sheen also donated his services for the Public Broadcasting Service production of *No Place to Hide*. He said, "I do it because, in my mind, I have no other choice when I feel strongly enough about something."

As his spirituality and social concerns grew, so did Martin's active involvement in political issues. In February of 1982, when Screen Actors Guild president Ed Asner took a stand against American military involvement in Central America, Sheen issued a public letter in several industry trade publications. It read:

> "Dear Ed,
> "I hate having to spend money for this letter as I'm sure we both agree it would be far better spent on the El Salvadoran relief effort. However, attention must also be paid to you personally in this regard. Thank you for accepting the responsibility most of us have conveniently chosen to ignore. I'm proud of your courage and deeply moved by your compassion. I'm proud to call you my president and my only regret is that I was unable to join you and my fellow actors in Washington, D.C., on President's Day.
> "Sincerely, Martin Sheen"

That paid advertisement earned Martin a lot of hate mail and even a death threat. But he still joined Asner in collecting funds for medical aid to El Salvador, and the two men have remained close friends.

In a *Los Angeles Times* interview, Sheen was quoted as saying, "I've been warned by a lot of people to keep my views to myself. But on that occasion I had to do what I did. I never want the time to come when I look back and feel ashamed. Courage, in my view, is the first virtue.''

"Courage leads to all other virtues," he expanded on another occasion. "But I've never experienced courage in myself. I've known it in other people; I know it when I see it. What is the hardest, most courageous thing to do in any given situation? Usually it amounts to simply telling the truth—both to yourself, and revealing it when called upon to do so. But basically you do this by your life. You live your courage. I don't qualify for that because if I did I'd probably be in a jail cell somewhere.''

Martin Sheen, however, has not flinched from the prospect of going to jail for his beliefs, and there are many who do not flinch at calling him courageous. But no amount of devotion to his causes would keep him too far away from his first love: acting.

Among Sheen's favorite projects, 1983's *Man, Woman, and Child* ranks about third behind *Badlands* and *Apocalypse Now*. Based on a novella by Erich Segal (who wrote *Love Story*), it's the tale of happily married college professor Bob Beckwith, who is suddenly confronted with the discovery that he has a ten-year-old son by a long-ago affair with a French woman. After the woman dies in an auto accident, the boy joins Beckwith, his wife, and two daughters (ages thirteen and nine) in the States for a get-acquainted visit. The visit strains Beckwith's marriage and tests everyone's's love for each other.

There was an unusual clause in Sheen's contract for this movie. He requested a one-and-a-half-hour lunch break during which he would do Hatha Yoga exercises with an instructor. Having found a health regime when recovering from his heart attack, Martin was not about to backslide. He combined good sense with his rediscovered interest in Eastern philosophies to keep himself in balance.

The reborn Catholic had by now comfortably integrated his church with an interest in Indian mysticism, an interest he had developed long before the filming of *Gandhi*. Sheen has studied at the ashram of Omraam Mikhael Aivanhov and has been healed by Bikram Choudry at The Yoga College of Indic Studies in Beverly Hills. Good health means balance in all areas: body, mind, and spirit. In the Sheen household, there are no cupboards full of junk food; the kitchen is stocked with natural food and vitamins. (Sheen did, however, start smoking again.)

In Stephen King's *The Dead Zone* for Paramount that same year, Martin played Greg Stillson, a maverick politician who becomes a moral focus for Christopher Walken's character, Johnny Smith, a young man who has developed eerie psychic powers during a long coma. Burt Lancaster was originally slated for the role, but he had not fully recuperated from open-heart surgery when the film moved into production earlier than first scheduled.

Martin's scenes were filmed at Niagara-on-the-Lake, Canada; in 1983, the population was 12,500 and the local unemployment rate was 21 percent. When candidate Stillson's outdoor political rally was filmed on the town common, 600 people lined up at 7:00 A.M.—right before Christmas—to apply to be extras. A lucky 250 were chosen. They were the patient, but usually freezing, folks who either huddled together for two nights at the gazebo shoot or cheered Sheen for a couple of days in support of his character's campaign. Martin was struck by the way that in spite of the Canadian winter temperatures, the extras maintained constant enthusiasm with hardly a complaint.

Sheen became the most popular man in town, getting to know the shopkeepers and even the postman. Of his character, he noted that Stillson was the kind of sleazy, immoral, and unprincipled type of politician he would dedicate himself to defeating.

The following year, Martin made another Stephen King adaptation, *Firestarter*. This turned out to be the first time author and actor met. King remembered the meeting well:

"I got down to North Carolina for only two days," he said. "I had dinner with Dino [de Laurentiis] and Martin and a friend of mine. The thing that I remember about Martin is that he is the most articulate man and the most knowledgeable actor on the subject of politics that I had ever met, with the exception of E.G. Marshall. Of course, the thing about E.G. is that he's pretty right-wing, a very conservative guy. And Martin is a nice counter to that; he's very liberal.

"He knew a lot about the Kennedys and the Kennedy administration. We talked about apartheid in South Africa. He's a very smart and very pleasant man. I was impressed by his intelligence and how many outside interests he has."

Martin played two characters that were born in Stephen King's imagination: a government agent on the run and and a corrupt politician. King found Martin's choice of roles interesting. "Martin told me he got a kick out of playing the kind of men he doesn't like. I personally think he deserved an Academy Award nomination for his Greg Stillson portrayal," King said. "There's one scene I had written where Stillson puts on a hard hat and throws out hot dogs to the audience, and gives this real down-home, country-boy speech. I couldn't imagine Martin Sheen doing it. But he pulled it off beautifully."

While Martin's career commands most of his time, he is always a devoted family man who takes time to be involved with his children's endeavors. Ramon, for instance, earned a small role as a photographer while visiting his dad on *The Dead Zone* location. Between projects, Martin visits his sons at work whenever he can.

To Martin, his children are more than an obligation or a responsibility or a joy. They are also a destiny. As he told *Vanity Fair*, "We pick our parents and children before birth. It's not an accident. Our children come to us to make up for past-life indiscretions. . . . They're holdovers from lifetimes we haven't yet solved. We've all been here before. Every lifetime is an attempt to get back to the Father.''

The greatest tribute he has made to his children, though, was this simple line: ''I love these people as friends.''

Nineteen-eighty-four turned out to be a particularly important one for Martin and Janet as parents. Both of them were extremely supportive when, in June of that year, Emilio made them grandparents for the first time. Although Emilio and the mother, Carey Salley, never wed, the Sheen home and hearts welcomed the baby boy, Taylor Levi. Later, in early December of the same year, Charlie's girlfriend of the time brought the first granddaughter, Cassandra, into the family.

It was also the year that Emilio made his commercial breakthrough in the film *Repo Man*. Martin would often stop by the set or production offices, offering support and encouragement, but never taking the role of backseat driver. Recalled Emilio's costar, Sy Richardson, ''We were hanging around the office, taking poster pictures for the film. Martin came in looking for Emilio and we just started talking. I'm not the kind of guy who runs up to another actor, introduces myself, and just starts talking. I maintain my space and stay there. But Martin walked right up to me and said, 'Hi. I've seen some of your rushes. You're very good. There are two or three guys in this film that I think will make it to stardom, Sy, and you're one of them.' My lip hit the floor! That really made my day—made my whole week, actually.''

''Martin is one of the nicest guys you could ever want to meet,'' Richardson added. ''He's sweet, easygoing, always telling jokes. No one is a stranger to him . . . and he's not as intense as you'd expect him to be from his films. *Emilio* is very intense. What you might expect from Martin, you get from Emilio.''

▪ 7 ▪

Activist Actor and More

THE SEEDS OF MARTIN SHEEN'S SOCIAL CONSCIENCE WERE planted in his youth, cultivated through his convictions, and blossomed as a result of his courage. Sheen is not an actor who became a star and then tacked on his name to a convenient cause; he's an activist whose excellence in his profession brings greater attention to the battles he fights for peace and human rights. Today, Martin is involved in the peace movement, the effort toward nuclear disarmament, the rights of the homeless, fighting American aggression in Central America, the struggle against apartheid in South Africa, and the AIDS crisis.

Close to Christmas in 1984, Sheen flew to Managua and spent several days in Nicaragua to observe the effects of U.S. involvement in Central America. "When I went, I asked the President [Reagan] permission to wish the people of Nicaragua—just those I would run into, not even the government, just the people I would meet on my

45

journey—a Merry Christmas. That's all I asked," Sheen said shortly after his visit.

"I wired the Secretary of State [Schultz] and I made the same request: 'Please, Mr. President, Mr. Secretary of State, allow me to wish the people of Nicaragua a Merry Christmas on your behalf.' And I didn't receive any response." Nor did he get a reply from the head of the National Security Council, Robert MacFarland.

Only after Sheen had returned did he find a letter from presidential advisor Admiral John Poindexter, postmarked "The White House." It included a copy of a speech the President had given earlier in the year to the joint session of Congress, and a history lesson from Admiral Poindexter. "He was very interested in peace in Nicaragua," Sheen remembered of Poindexter's letter, "and it would come if the Sandinistas would stop invading and threatening their neighbors and being such good friends with the Soviets and the Cubans; if they would just behave themselves there would be peace."

Sheen was deeply disappointed by the actions and reactions of his elected officials (even though they were individuals he did not personally choose). As he told the *Los Angeles Reader*, "I still wanted to believe that the people that run my government are better than me. I mean, I really want to believe that," he said.

While in Nicaragua, Sheen made a statement of solidarity by donating blood through the local Red Cross. "Our American brothers were taking blood, and we wanted to have a sign of giving it back. I gave my blood in the name of my brother, Ronald Reagan."

Martin Sheen has said that he considers Father Daniel Berrigan to be the most courageous person he has ever met. He says he doesn't consider himself very courageous at all. How can he go around, he wondered, "wearing Gucci loafers when I should be in jail for committing acts of civil disobedience. I've been in jail a few times for misbehaving, and I belonged there, but never for a righteous reason.'' By now, many of Martin's friends and colleagues in the peace movement had been jailed for their beliefs. He watched as his "brothers" were arrested for attempting to disarm a missile silo.

"Those are the peacemakers the government calls terrorists," said Martin. But "I'm too governed by fear to go to prison. I haven't cooperated with God's grace."

But as time went on, Martin contributed more and more money and effort to his beliefs.

In March of 1987, Martin organized the "Grate American Sleepout" in Washington, D.C. Joined by fellow film actors Brian Dennehy and Dennis Quaid, daytime star Grant Cramer, and more than a dozen congressmen, Sheen huddled with supporters and street people over two steam vents in front of the Library of Congress. The idea was to share the plight of America's homeless, people who could not find warmth in their city except that which was regurgitated from its underground tunnels. The demonstration was in support of a bill that would provide $500 million in government relief for these people.

Said Sheen, "We are the government, and if Americans were truly made aware of what's going on in this country in their name—with their taxpaying money—they would object and they would respond. Americans are good and decent people, but they're not aware. . . .

"Our government expropriates two hundred million dollars *per day* in maintaining a useless nuclear arsenal, while less than one percent of the federal budget is spent on low-income housing. The whole world watches while forty-six human beings starve to death worldwide every sixty seconds."

On July 7, 1987 Sheen was arrested on trespassing charges—then issued a summons and released—when he and two dozen other demonstrators protested nuclear weapons at the Riverside Research Institute in New York City.

At the time, he told the *New York Post*: "The death being planned here—the work on missile accuracy and Star Wars—is done in all our names. I am here to say 'Not in my name.'

"The millions of dollars that will be spent on Star Wars [the Strategic Defense Initiative], a dangerous escalation of the arms race, is a theft from the poor. It must be stopped."

On July 15, 1987 a small group of anti-nuclear protesters, including Martin Sheen, gathered in front of the RAND Corporation's Santa Monica, California headquarters. Sheen believed that advance planning for a potential first-strike initiative was being done at the RAND think tank. He told *USA Today*, "This is a place where the end of the world is planned. We can be creative and we can be destructive and, for the last forty years, we've been destructive."

Sheen was also arrested in early November of that year in Mercury, Nevada at an anti-nuclear demonstration during which protesters spilled nails at the entrance to the Nevada test site, hoping to block entry by vehicles. More than 200 people in all were arrested and charged with misdemeanor trespass. All were released. The demonstration was sponsored by the Los Angeles and Las Vegas chapters of the Catholic Worker, a group Martin had first become active in two decades before, and was honoring what would have been the ninetieth birthday of Dorothy Day, who had founded a movement to promote peace and help the poor in the thirties.

A few days after his release in Nevada, Martin was arrested again in Washington, D.C. for trying to interfere with the erection of a fence that was designed to keep the homeless from taking refuge in a subway station near the White House. Sheen and homeless activist Mitch Snyder were charged with unlawful entry.

"The last year has become more intense," said Sheen to a *USA Today* reporter. "And yet it has been the most rewarding of my life. I hate the arrest, the booking, the dehumanization of the whole judicial process. I'm the biggest coward I know. I feel faint, I want to throw up. But I cannot *not* be active anymore. I want to be anonymous, but I cannot.''

As if his list of causes and participation is not already long enough, Sheen is also actively involved with the Special Olympics, held each June in Los Angeles. An event that encourages athletic achievement among young people with mental and physical handicaps, it's one of the only competitions Martin Sheen embraces and approves of wholeheartedly.

▪ 8 ▪

Keeping On

As Sheen approached what many would consider middle age—but what was to Martin simply a new era of growth and change—he continued to attack his career with gusto. Unlike many actors in their prime who refuse to do anything but movies, theater, or specific television projects, Martin continued to do it all. He even did commercials, sometimes simply voice-overs, on radio as well as television. That's Martin Sheen you hear talking when Michael J. Fox is crawling out the window to fetch a Diet Pepsi for his pretty neighbor. And that's Martin Sheen extolling the virtues of the Toyota Camry racing through the countryside.

Work is work, but when it comes to a big-screen portrayal—a role that would involve his soul—Martin was at a point where he could choose to play only characters that appealed to his inner sensibilities. He had to find a certain satisfaction, a certain humanity, in the people he portrayed. "You have to be human," he told the *Hollywood Reporter*. "You have to respond to the humanity of the

51

work. Every work will generally reflect some part of who you are, where you come from, what you stand for. No matter what character you play, there's always going to be some sort of personal projection into that character. Some part of yourself is going to come through. That's what makes it so worthwhile.''

Despite the recognized quality of his work in all areas, Sheen still refused to accept any involvement in acting awards. In 1985 he received another Emmy nomination, this time for his supporting role in *The Atlanta Child Murders*. One more time, he requested that the Academy of Television Arts and Sciences remove his name from the ballot; the program producers had entered it without his knowledge. The Academy granted his request.

"Competition in the arts," he stressed yet again, "is really at odds with what you're trying to do. It takes a group of people, a community of people, to present anything in the performing arts. You can't do it on your own. Picking out specific people divides them from the effort it takes to be successful.''

It was during this period that Martin watched not one but two sons mature as actors and even stars. But he is sensitive to the harsh glare of the spotlight, and loathe to see his children endure the transition from "actor" to "celebrity." When Charlie became so popular in the wake of *Platoon*, Martin said, "We're delighted for him. But that much success for anyone in anything is not healthy. . . . It's madness for him right now. You want to go someplace with him? It's a public gathering. My heart goes out to him.

"I have to confess that I advised Charlie not to do *Platoon*. It was just so violent, and there was no heroism. I had no doubt that he would be successful, but I thought it would take ten or twelve years.''

Likewise, he said, "I was pleased that Emilio chose a creative profession, but saddened because I knew the pain he was in for . . . the pain of exposing yourself—to do in public what everyone else does in private. For a while, it seemed he would go to college and study forestry. But he decided to become an actor, and went after that in a very focused and concrete way.''

Martin's work in acting continued, and 1986 brought him a chance to fuse his sociopolitical and acting instincts in the television movie *Samaritan*, a biography of the homeless activist in whose company Sheen would later be arrested. Mitch Snyder was so devoted to the cause of the homeless that he had recently fasted for a total of eighty-four days to dramatize their plight.

"Of all the people in my life that I have really envied—and there are just a handful of them—Mitch Snyder is one," said Martin. "He is in full possession of his soul, which is what I would like to be in possession of. I'm sure all of us would. He has transcended the image of what it means to be a person—to really be a person."

It was also in 1986 that Martin won an Emmy—no doubt having been too distracted to withdraw his name from competition in time. Or perhaps it was because this was both a departure and a homecoming for him; the award was for directing, not acting, and one of the young actors he was directing was his daughter, Renee. The project was an ABC Afterschool Special called *Babies Having Babies*, and Renee played a teenaged unwed mother. (It is pure coincidence that at the same time, Carey Salley was giving birth to Emilio's youngest—and Martin's third grandchild—Paloma Estevez.)

By 1987, Martin Sheen was able to enjoy the left-handed compliment of being recognized as "Charlie and Emilio's dad." Where once both boys were identified in print as being sired by Sheen, now it seemed that their fame was eclipsing his own—which was fine as far as he was concerned, since he had worked happily at the top of his profession for two decades without ever requiring "household name" status to satisfy him.

When Martin made *The Believers* for director John Schlesinger in 1987, the first thing moviegoers would exclaim was, "He looks just like his kids! And he's so young!" Martin, forty-seven at the time, was able to convincingly play the father of a grade-schooler; it goes to show that a healthy regimen does work.

The Believers cast Sheen as Cal Jamison, a psychologist who gets caught up in a police investigation involving pagan ritual, murder, and madness. Martin was in London working on the play *The Normal Heart* at the Royal Court Theatre when producer-director Schlesinger visited him backstage. Sheen found it easy to relate to the character of Jamison because, "like him, I'm a Roman Catholic, a concerned father, someone who respects the beliefs of others—but dismisses the supernatural."

In preparation for his role, he went to the library and read books about Santeria, an obscure religion that blends Catholicism and the Yoruban faith of Nigeria. Historically, as slaves adapted to their new lives in Haiti, Cuba, Jamaica, and Central America, they combined the gods of their ancestors with the saints of their Catholic masters. It was that link to Catholicism that fascinated Sheen.

Martin also took the time to conduct long conversations with a psychiatric service doctor who specialized in the mental pressures of dangerous occupations, like police work. "I wasn't attempting to become Cal Jamison," he told reporters. "I tend to work the other way around. I was trying to find him in me."

From an actor's point of view, *The Believers* could not have been more challenging; Martin's emotions ranged from grief, shock, and terror to rage, compassion, tenderness, and courage. *The Believers*, however, was in many ways too much of a roller-coaster ride to achieve widespread popularity. Said movie reviewer Leonard Maltin,

"This well-crafted film knows how to manipulate its audience, but shows no mercy, either."

His next major role again gave Martin the chance to play a character with whom he could feel empathy. As the father—and conscience—of wheeler-dealer Bud Fox in *Wall Street*, he played a working-class hero and got to be dad to his own son, Charlie. *Wall Street* reunited Charlie Sheen and director Oliver Stone, and gave a big chunk of the spotlight to a member of yet another Hollywood dynasty: Michael Douglas, who was deliciously demonic as the power-hungry Gordon Gekko. Joe Fox, the union man who understood what it meant to work with his hands, served as a Greek chorus to the money-grubbing paper-shufflers of the stock exchange.

"The rich have been doing it to the poor since the beginning of time," said Martin, a line both in character and from the man. "The only difference between the pyramids and the Empire State Building is that the Egyptians didn't have unions."

Wall Street did not earn either the money or the respect that Stone's earlier *Platoon* had, but it was worthwhile for Martin because it gave him the opportunity to work with Charlie. And he found it possible to get involved with his kin off-camera, too. It was while he was shooting *Wall Street* that Martin was involved in that demonstration outside the Riverside Research Institute, and Charlie came along. Charlie, however, stayed far enough away from the action to avoid arrest.

The younger Sheen told journalist Tom Green that his father had actually requested that he get arrested in the incident, too, but Charlie didn't feel it was appropriate. "I said, 'No, but I'll come down there with you.' I walked him to the paddy wagon and met him at the station. I was right there for him.

"I understand basically what he's out there for," continued Charlie, "but he's gone far beyond the surface of things. He's into the deeper stages. And I don't want to get caught with my foot in my mouth.''

Charlie and Emilio both have received from their father a legacy not only of talent and self-expression, but of philosophy and social conscience that will become woven into the fabric of their futures. And both of them are being escalated onto a plateau of visibility so high and so fast that, when each gets in touch with his innermost beliefs—as happened to their father in his late thirties—the result will surely be explosive.

■ 9 ■

Number One Son of Sheen

EMILIO ESTEVEZ WAS BORN IN NEW YORK ON MAY 12, 1962 and was raised on Manhattan's Upper West Side. Calling it less than the best of neighborhoods would be an understatement: When he was only six, Emilio was mugged by a knife-wielding twelve-year-old in the lobby of his family's apartment building.

The incident remained clear in Emilio's mind even in 1985, when he described it for a *Seventeen* magazine reporter. It was, he recalled, exactly twenty-six cents that the robber stole; that's how much he saved up regularly to pay for a hot dog and a cream soda from the street vendor down the block.

As Martin's fortunes grew, so did the family's security—financial and physical. Dad often used to walk Emilio to school, and later enrolled him in a private academy. But Emilio's independent (some might say contrary) streak was already exhibiting itself in the earliest grades. One day he walked out of the private school where classes were conducted in French and never went back. "I couldn't handle the uniform," was his explanation.

In 1968 his dad was cast in *Catch-22* and happily moved the family west. Perhaps inspired by the sea breezes and beach landscapes, the seven-year-old started to write short stories and poems, because "the spirit moved me." He told one interviewer that this "spirit" gave him more direction than any number of English teachers or writing manuals. "You can be taught within certain parameters," said Emilio, "but I don't think anyone can really teach you creative writing."

Among his first serious attempts was an original episode he submitted (in pencil, on lined paper) to Rod Serling's *Night Gallery* TV series. Emilio was all of eight at the time, certainly a record of some sort in the annals of the television Writers Guild. That slightly premature effort earned him his first rejection slip, but did not deter him from experimenting with more of his own projects. By the time he was nine, the precocious grade-schooler was well aware of the benefits of writing, directing, and producing his own material.

While off on location in Ireland for *Catholics*, Martin bought the kids a home-movie-camera set-up. When the family came home to Malibu, that Super-8 equipment was all Emilio and his band of beach buddies—Chad and Rob Lowe, Chris and Sean Penn—needed to begin their film careers. By the time Emilio was thirteen, he had advanced to sound equipment, and his writing became an even more important part of the productions.

One of Emilio and Sean Penn's schoolmates, Ann Sonnenshein, remembered the group of nascent movie moguls: "They were really very creative about it. I'm not at all surprised that they're all involved in filmmaking today."

Not surprisingly, Sonnenshein still remembers both Sean and Emilio well. After all, she's reminded of them every time she walks into the supermarket and scans the newsracks.

"They were both 'very Malibu,' " she said. "Both were blond and tanned. Sean even won surfing contests in the ninth grade. And he was active in government during junior high. So was I, and I guess that's one of the reasons we hung out together at school."

Emilio may not be reminded of Ann in every supermarket checkout line, but he too remembers those days. "I was a beach bum," he said flatly. "I went to the beach every day, hanging out with the surfers . . . the old fifties surfboards—twelve feet long, made of wood, and with a tail-fin rudder—so big and easy to surf, you could have a cup of coffee on them."

Sonnenshein described Sean and Emilio as two halves of a whole, buddies to the end. "Sean was very polite, very quiet. He had a sweet demeanor. We lost track of each other during high school. It was a much bigger school. Emilio looked the same during high school, and he even looks pretty similar today from what I see of him on the screen. Emilio and Sean had their own friendship. I knew them at school, but didn't socialize with them at home. They were Malibu; I wasn't. Sean . . . when I hear of his aggression it really surprises me. He changed so much. Emilio seems much more consistent."

One thing that certainly has remained consistent within Emilio is his passion for movies and moviemaking. "I love film," he has enthused to reporters. "I see everything: the garbage, the great films, a lot of oldies. I think you can learn even from bad films. You see how you would have done it differently, to make it better."

At thirteen, Emilio spent some time in Rome when his father was acting in *The Cassandra Crossing*. He was fourteen when he spent four months with his father in the Philippines during the filming of *Apocalypse Now*. But even as a teenager, he was an old hand on the movie set; he'd been hanging around them since he was a tadpole. Martin was always adamant that his movie contracts include six airline tickets to wherever the location was so that his family could spend as much time together as possible.

But it was during those four months of *Apocalypse*, amid the family havoc of extreme stress and illness, that Emilio got his first acting job. He was only an extra and his turn as a messenger boy ended up on the cutting-room floor. But it was a start. And, as it turned out, it was while swigging beer in the seedier areas of Manila that he established a relationship that would lead to his first play; within those dank rooms he became acquainted with the Vietnam vet who formed the inspiration for an original stage offering, written and produced by Emilio in his final year of high school.

The first-born Estevez's academic record sports many A's with a smattering of B's and only the fewest C's through junior and senior high school. His lowest grades were consistently in math, and once he got a D in English. (But did any of the other kids in that class have a rejection slip from *Night Gallery*?)

As his over-the-ears, surfer-blond hair gradually became darker and shorter, Emilio found himself acting in most of the plays produced at his junior high school: *The Dumb Waiter, Hello Out There, Bye Bye Birdie*. At the start of senior high he paid a bit more attention to athletics, which widened his circle of acquaintances—or perhaps potential character studies is more accurate.

He ran track ("so I was in with all the black dudes"), played soccer ("I knew the Hispanics and Latinos"), knew all the surfers ("because I grew up in Malibu"), and got along very well with the brainy students (because he usually received good grades.) During his final year, he decided he was "too short" to be a sports star, so he turned his attention back to the drama department. But the sophisticated student just couldn't get behind the literary chestnuts that were being mounted by the school that year. Who can get turned on by a high school production when you've been on the set of the latest Francis Ford Coppola blockbuster? So Emilio wrote his own play, *Echoes of an Era*, had pal Sean Penn direct it, and invited classmates to come watch it.

The play was based on the experiences of the Vietnam vet Emilio had met in Manila, a soldier who had been badly wounded and left for dead in a field. Eventually, the GI made it back to the United States, only to have a very difficult time adjusting to the life he had left behind years before. The story was not unique for its day, but it was real and it was certainly not the usual fodder for a teenaged playwright.

Schoolmate Cara Poston remembered the play well. "It was definitely the best production I ever saw at school. We were impressed not just with Emilio's acting in it, but by the fact that he wrote it, too.

"Emilio was definitely into the drama department," Poston recalled. "It has never surprised any of us who knew him back then that he would be doing so well today. From seeing his work through school, it was taken for granted—even expected—that he would do very well in acting and in the movie business in general. Of the three brothers—Emilio, Ramon, and Charlie—Emilio was definitely the most outgoing and the most popular with everyone."

During that period, Emilio also acted in a short film entitled *Meet Mr. Bomb*, an anti-nuclear parody of the "duck and cover" films of the fifties. Later, when draft registration was reinstated in 1980, Emilio risked a five-year jail term and a $10,000 fine when he refused to register, and he was also active in the antiregistration movement. Luckily, there were no negative consequences for him. The courts didn't bother to prosecute and his parents were on his side. Sociopolitical activism is another inherited trait in this family.

Although Emilio at one time entertained the "romantic idea" of becoming a foreign correspondent (before his firsthand contact with reporters, that is), he knew he enjoyed being onstage or in front of the cameras just as much as writing. He started going out on interviews and auditions when he was sixteen, and landed his first professional stage role at seventeen, while still a senior in high school. It was a part in *Mr. Roberts* at the Burt Reynolds Dinner Theater in Jupiter, Florida, where his dad was also on the playbill. But the cast list wasn't to read "Sheen & Sheen" . . . nor would it, until Martin worked alongside another son years later.

Emilio decided to use his family name, Estevez, as his professional tag. After all, he had used it all through high school and it simply felt right. "Besides," he said, "Emilio Sheen sounds stupid anyway. Emilio Estevez sounds more romantic." And there's the fact that the name change set him apart from his father. Emilio has admitted that he was cast in that particular role through the offices of his dad, but always felt uneasy about having done so and never wanted to do so again if he could help it.

"That was the only job my dad ever placed me in," said Emilio later. "We were well into production by the time I acquitted myself of the sin of casting nepotism."

Back at Santa Monica High, Emilio resettled easily into garden-variety teenagerhood, seasoned actor though he was by now. So much the perfect All-American boy, Emilio earned the title of Prom King ("the most embarrassing moment of my life!") in his final year.

English teacher Berkley Blatz recalled: "Each year the senior class invited one of the male and one of the female teachers to their prom, and I was there that year. Emilio was elected by his peers as the King of the Prom and I played a small part in that drama. I got to place the crown on the head of the Queen, while the female teacher placed the crown on Emilio's head. Emilio accepted the honor with good grace, but it wasn't as if he had been campaigning for it. And I don't think he was truly overjoyed about the whole thing. He struck me as being a little bit shy.''

What stood out most about this fabulously talented youngster? Well, according to Cara Poston, ''He was noted for having the 'prettiest hair.' '' Fact is, Emilio's high school years were filled with academic, athletic, professional, and social success. He was the kind of student who always handed reports in on time and did extra assignments. He could hang out with the guys and match them beer for beer, and still be consistently in top shape to win track meets. When it came time for baby brother Charlie to attend Emilio's alma mater, the younger sibling discovered that it can be tough to compete with a near-perfect predecessor's memory.

After school, Emilio went full-steam into acting as a profession. His first movie role was, fittingly, an ABC Afterschool Special entitled *17 and Going Nowhere*. Then followed a television role in *Making the Grade* and, later in 1980, ''To Climb a Mountain'' with his father—an episode of *Insight*, the syndicated TV program produced as a dramatic mini-sermon by the Catholic Paulist order.

His nineteenth year was an eventful one; in 1981, he was witness to the poverty and spiritual zeal of India when he accompanied Martin on location for *Gandhi*—and witness to his father's spiritual rebirth as well. He saw his parents' marriage become stronger than ever, healed from the separation that occurred after *Apocalypse*. Images of India would continue to haunt both father and son. For Emilio, they would soon pale somewhat against the excitement of his first feature-film role.

Tex was to be the first of three movies Emilio would make based on Susan E. Hinton's novels. It starred Matt Dillon, Jim Metzler, Meg Tilly, Ben Johnson, and Bill McKinney; Emilio's role was very small. Just before production on *Tex* started in Oklahoma in 1981, Emilio also screen-tested for another Hinton novel-to-film adaptation, *The Outsiders* (scheduled to go into production a year later).

Just about any other young actor would have set out for his first movie location with an Instamatic camera, stamped postcards, and a blank notebook/diary. When *this* film impresario-to-be arrived on the *Tex* location site, he had his script and all four Hinton novels (including *Rumble Fish* and *That Was Then . . . This Is Now*) under his arm.

Emilio read them back to back, and was immediately "deeply, deeply affected" by the last one, the story of a troubled high school senior. Already looking towards the future, Emilio managed to option the rights to the novel and, with pal Tom Cruise, wrote the first draft of a screenplay in fourteen days. By January of 1984 he had completed the polished script.

Between filming *Tex* in late 1981 and tackling his next big-screen part in *The Outsiders* at the end of 1982, Estevez added several more television roles to his resumé: an NBC-TV thriller, *Nightmares*, in which he played a driven video-game addict; and an ABC-TV movie, *In the Custody of Strangers* with Jane Alexander, in which he portrayed a sixteen-year-old drunk driver who spends six weeks in jail. The latter was well-received by the critics and also featured Martin Sheen.

Emilio has, on numerous occasions, admitted that he's "competitive, stubborn, driven, and a very intense individual." Once his career started to roll, he intended to make certain that it would continue to gain momentum and stature. He made it clear, too, that he had no intention of remaining in his famous father's shadow.

At the time, however, Emilio chose to share the small-screen spotlight with his father in the ABC-TV movie. A few years later, Emilio explained his feelings to actor Sy Richardson: "A lot of people think that my father got this job and gave me this role. But it was the other way around. I got the part, and I went to my father and asked if he'd do this film with me. And he asked me why. I said, 'I don't know how long either of us will be here, but this is a time that you and I can actually work together, and I would like to share this moment with you.' And my father agreed to do the movie.''

Emilio often feels conflict within when analyzing his feelings about following in his father's footsteps. On the one hand, he doesn't want to be seen as a clone of his daddy, or an upstart who has had doors opened for him because of his family connections. On the other hand, he admires his father's talent and has learned a great deal from him, which he would be foolish (not to mention ungrateful) to deny.

"When you're young, you want to do what your father does,'' said Emilio. "As I got older, I wanted to make it a reality.'' And as he got older, he also wanted to separate his reality from Martin's. Calling himself a "stubborn Taurus,'' Emilio said, "My father's a great man, but it was time to be on my own.'' And he stated elsewhere, "It's a sensitive subject, being Martin Sheen's son. The more I disassociate myself, the more the public will see Emilio Estevez. . . . Anything I can consciously do to make a separation from my father, I will do.''

Although Emilio has "incredible love and respect'' for his father, and admitted that "having an actor-father is more valuable than anything that can be taught,'' Emilio has also stated: "As far as advice from him goes, well, the business has changed so much since the time he started that things don't quite apply. He's into his family and removed from the industry—and me, I've jumped in with both feet. I guess I'm trying to find a tactful way of saying I don't take his advice.

"I made a conscious decision not to ride on the coattails of my father's success when I started acting . . . I swore to myself that if I made it, it would be through drive, ambition, and hard work. I wanted to know I got it that way and not because of my bloodlines. And I think there's no question why I got where I am today.''

The father knows his son well. Martin commented in an interview, ''Emilio's fought for his independence, and I appreciate the way he feels. My heart says, 'Do more for him,' but I have to wait for him to call me. I'd love to work with him all the time.''

▪ 10 ▪

Think Big, Bigger, Biggest

With the release of *The Outsiders* in early 1983, Emilio found himself among some of the sexiest young actors on the Hollywood scene, all who have individually gone on to major film success and heartthrob status: Tom Cruise, Matt Dillon, Rob Lowe, Patrick Swayze, C. Thomas Howell, and Ralph Macchio. None of this was expected back in 1982, however, when *Tex* had not yet been released and S.E. Hinton was a name known only to teenage bookworms.

The movie project grew from a short story written by schoolgirl Susan Hinton in 1965, after a friend of hers was beaten up on the way home from class. It was published as a novel in 1967 with the author using S.E. Hinton as a byline . . . in case readers (and Viking Press) would be put off by a "mere" girl. At any rate, the book was an immediate must-read for young adults.

Then, in 1980, producer Francis Ford Coppola received a letter at his Zoetrope Studios from the librarian of the Lone Star Junior High School in Fresno, California, stating that the faculty and students of her school had nominated him to make a movie out of this special book. A hand-signed petition from the students was attached. How could he refuse?

The Outsiders is a story of kids from the wrong side of the tracks, the "greasers," in conflict with the affluent "socs" (pronounced "soshes"), a conflict that leads to tragedy of Shakespearean proportions. Emilio played a greaser, Two-Bit Matthews, a role originally intended for Cruise.

"I grew up in a borderline neighborhood," explained Hinton. "I played with the 'greasers' but I got put in classes with the 'socs.' " Being in the middle helped the author understand both groups. And, given Emilio's ability throughout high school to get along with classmates in every socioeconomic group, it's clear why the story appealed to him.

Emilio also enjoyed his second opportunity to work with Coppola, since the director did not have that much direct contact with Emilio on the set of *Apocalypse Now*. "Francis has children of his own, so he understood us," Emilio said. "He let us go on our own. The only direction he ever gave me was, 'We're still rolling—do something funny.' He pretty much stayed out of the way. He made the film for fourteen-year-old kids and for nobody else, and that's who it ultimately appealed to—it had no crossover."

That became painfully clear. For as successful as *The Outsiders* was in novel form, its movie reviews were mediocre at best. Vincent Canby stated his opinion in *The New York Times*: "Like *Tex*, a far more successful, far less pretentious film, *The Outsiders* means to be about the world as it appears to teenagers . . . it's another of Coppola's inflated attempts at myth-making, it's a melodramatic kid-film with the narrative complexity of *The Three Bears* and a high body count."

Rolling Stone critic Michael Sragow felt it "turned out to be a movie that gives adolescence a bad name." And Rex Reed said, "*The Outsiders* is a pretentious, disjointed tearjerker that takes a simple story (so basic it practically evaporates) and pumps it up to the size and status of *Gone With the Wind*."

Emilio didn't bear the brunt of these negative reviews; in fact he was hardly mentioned in the majority of press about the film. To make matters worse, another project was not on the horizon. He didn't work for five months after the movie was released.

"I had expectations," he admitted to an interviewer several years later, "just as when I made *In the Custody of Strangers* and then didn't work for six months. I just couldn't land a major film. I was depressed, with no one to really talk to. The girl I was seeing was in Europe, and my old man was working. I wasn't living at home."

In 1983, Oliver Stone offered Emilio the role of Private First Class Chris Taylor in *Platoon*, but financing for the project was incomplete. Back in 1983, no one quite understood the importance of Stone's epic production; the Vietnam War was commercial poison, and a topic best left buried. So while Stone continued to pull his financial backing together, Emilio went to work on his next feature project.

Repo Man was an odd duck of a small-budget picture, financed in part by former musical Monkee Michael Nesmith and directed by a British lawyer-turned-UCLA-film-student named Alex Cox. Distributed hesitantly by Universal, *Repo Man* cast Emilio as a young Los Angeles punker who becomes the protégé of a crusty car repossessor played by cult actor Harry Dean Stanton. Actor Sy Richardson, who was once a repo man himself, costarred in the movie, which garnered mixed reviews from critics but has since become an extremely popular video classic.

"He's a nice guy, Emilio," Richardson said. "He's

friendly, but distant . . . I loved watching Emilio work. He's very professional, very intense, but he wasn't arrogant, wasn't egotistical.

"I think ninety percent of this business is being able to go on the set, know your lines, do what you do to the best of your ability, and leave. He was very good at it; I can't even remember him blowing a line. Most of us blow lines every now and again, but I can't remember ever seeing him do it. Most of the time he stayed by himself, like he was always preparing, always making sure that he was on the money. A lot of us want to be here until we roll over and croak, so we're always checking and working and watching."

Despite being older and more experienced in his craft, Richardson found that he could learn a great deal from Emilio, who was a natural at both the artistic and logistical sides of his profession. "I watched and listened. And I picked up on his ideas. He would get real quiet and look directly into someone's eyes, and never leave that eye contact—it's called neurolinguistic programming."

Or more simply, it can be called intensity, a quality that forces your attention on the speaker. Richardson described the first day he met Emilio: "We were in a room with a long table, and all the principal characters were sitting there. This young guy started the dialogue. I didn't know who he was; all I knew was that I had never heard an actor read a script as quietly as he read. You could barely hear what he was saying. I was leaning over the table listening to him—but I realized that, listening to him, I was paying close attention. I could hear the inflections in his voice. I didn't know if I was believing him or if I was just engrossed in hearing him, but it worked."

Richardson also recalled that even at twenty-one, Emilio was seasoned enough to think on his feet. One ad-lib stands out in his mind, the time when Harry Dean Stanton's character, Bud, is giving Otto (Estevez) a hard time.

The hard-nosed senior repossessor is explaining to the buzz-cut kid that normally, when someone gets in his way, he gets his head broken—or something equally as unappealing. With a smirk, Otto takes his beer and defiantly pours it out on the floor as a response. Or so the scene was written. But during one particular take, no one had noticed that the prop can of beer had not been set out.

Said Richardson, "This time Emilio doesn't have a beer. So he reaches into his pocket and hands him a dime. Harry Dean just looks at him for a second, because he's waiting for something else, then asks, 'What's this for?' And Emilio coolly says, 'Go call somebody who gives a fuck.'

"Everyone on the set just died. Alex [Cox, the director] was rolling on the floor. Emilio was really there. They didn't have the beer for him, and he had to come up with something, and he sure did. Harry Dean stood there thinking about it for a moment and then burst out laughing. Alex just shook his head and said, 'Boy, I wish I could use this!' It was really funny."

It was clear to everyone that Estevez could hold his own ground in his chosen field. It was also evident to Richardson that Emilio would become a talented producer-director. "Oh yes," Richardson enthused, "he has a lot of determination. I remember, when we finished *Repo Man*, I asked him what he wanted to do next. He said, 'Sy, for the next two to four years, I want to work. I've got a lot of things I want to do, and I've got them all written down. I'm going to do them.' And this kid's been working ever since. He knew in his mind what he wanted to do. Everyone else was talking about taking a vacation for a month, going off to regroup, but he said, 'No, I don't have the time. I have things I have to do by a certain age.' "

Of Emilio the man—as opposed to Emilio the actor—Richardson was struck by his spiritual nature and his sincere family-orientation. "Every time he sees me, the first thing he asks me is 'How is your son?' This is more important to him than how I am or how I feel. He asks how my son is, how the family unit is because he knows I'm a single parent.''

This emphasis on family never seemed to go the other way, remembered Richardson. He didn't recall Emilio ever talking about his own mother or a girlfriend. But Richardson felt that Emilio has a great respect for women in general. ''One day when we were looping [recording voice tracks], someone came into the room with three or four women. Emilio took note and quietly asked, 'Isn't that guy married?' And just by his asking that, I realized that he has a respect for women. It bothered him to see this guy with these ladies, knowing he has a wife somewhere.

''I never saw a lot of girls around him,'' Richardson continued. ''I know he had a girlfriend, and she came to the set once. With most of these young guys, you always see a lot of women around them. Not him. Emilio came to the set to work. He had this big truck, and the day that his girlfriend came around, they sat in his truck and talked instead of going into one of the trailers. I don't know if they sat there so that everybody could see. . . . Sometimes when guys get in their trailers and get the ladies in there, many things can happen. Maybe he didn't want people to think that he was doing something.''

The character of Otto turned out to be one of Emilio's favorite roles. ''I played him with a lot of dry, ugly humor, but funny. Look at the world we live in,'' he challenged a reporter, ''it's totally ridiculous. You just have to laugh at every situation life hands you.''

And although he is not as nihilistic a fellow as punk-rocker Otto (in fact, he had to study then-punk-loving brother Ramon for the right moves), he has since admitted that ''I have a kind of nihilistic point of view. I'm into making films that are realistic and not fluff. When you deal with reality, you're dealing with a lot of serious problems. We could be sitting here now and be vaporized by a nuclear weapon, by accident. That's reality. A man could walk in here and blow us all away with a machine gun. That's reality. Life does not end happily ever after.''

After *Repo Man*, Emilio shrugged aside the depression he had felt earlier. "Deep down," he said, "I knew my life would change. I just had to believe in myself, stop feeling like a loser, and be more positive." The change of attitude worked. Emilio's next film brought him to the attention of fans and critics alike.

The Breakfast Club, filmed in early 1984 for 1985 release, was to be the first of a string of teen movie successes by Chicagoan John Hughes. The director had already made *Sixteen Candles* to some acclaim, but no one was prepared for the impact of this unusual stage play of a movie. It had a cast of seven main characters and was shot on a single soundstage at an actual high school. *The Breakfast Club* tells the emotional story of five students thrown together during a Saturday morning detention session, a session that becomes a day of soul-searching and revelation for them all. Ally Sheedy, who played "basket case" Allison Reynolds, told the unit publicist: "It was a very special experience. We were an ensemble cast who became a very close-knit group. I felt like there was so much warmth and caring that I trusted everyone to open up."

Judd Nelson played rocker John Bender, the disdainful outsider; Anthony Michael Hall was the straight-A student Brian Johnson; Molly Ringwald was the pampered princess, Claire Standish. Emilio played Andy Clark, a star wrestler who doesn't know how to think for himself.

"I took the role because I never had the chance to play a jock or model son before," Emilio explained during production. "I've always played hoodlums. In fact, when I first read the script I saw myself as the punk, John Bender. But then Andy grew on me. He has a lot of turmoil.

Everyone rides him. It's an intolerable burden. He really wants to break out but he's conditioned not to. If a wrestler lets down his defense, he loses. So he can't and won't be vulnerable. People say they love Andy but they really don't. He's just a trophy they can show off.''

The lone grown-ups in the cast were John Kapelos, playing the janitor, Carl; and Paul Gleason as the smarmy, unsympathetic ''authority figure,'' the dean of students, Richard Vernon.

Veteran character-actor Gleason remembered Emilio as being ''very dedicated to whatever project is at hand. During the shooting of *Breakfast Club*, he played a wrestler, so I'd see him working out with weights every morning, sometimes between scenes, and sometimes after work, too. He was really into creating a good sense of reality about that character. And, as if that weren't enough, he was also writing a screenplay at the time. Adapting a Hinton novel, *That Was Then . . . This Is Now*.''

''I think the Sheens are a wonderful family,'' continued Gleason. ''I know Emilio and Charlie and think their parents, Martin and Janet, did a wonderful job in raising those kids. Martin is such an honest and sincere man. He's a wonderful actor and as an individual, is very socially conscious and involved. The boys have really learned a lot from his example.

''During the making of *Breakfast Club* we all hung around together and I got to know all the kids. We had a lot of fun kibbitzing around. Emilio was the leader of those kids. They really looked up to him. He has a leadership quality. He held the most respect. And of course, the girls—Ally and Molly—liked him a lot because he's a great guy, a terrific human being. It may sound effusive, but Emilio is really a very, very good guy. He's not a phony. My daughter, Shannon, who was thirteen at the time, was with us on that location. She reacted to his honesty, too.''

Gleason pointed out the traits that struck him about Emilio: "He's talented; he's gifted. He was lucky enough to have been raised in a wonderful family. And he's worked hard for his success. Best of all, Emilio takes nothing for granted and he's not the kind of young man to be self-destructive. He has a lot of solid self-respect and is not the kind of person to destroy his life and his talent through drugs or alcohol or any other destructive habit. That's highly commendable, and very refreshing in this business."

"Professionally, he's a Renaissance kid," Gleason enthused. "Emilio can work in front of the camera or in many areas behind it. With the success of *Stakeout*, I think he'll be getting a lot of offers and we'll see more and more of him on the movie screen. It's fun to act, and I think he enjoys that. But he's so talented, he'll be developing his own projects as a director and writer, too. Emilio's very eclectic."

• 11 •

That Was That, This Is It

SUSAN HINTON WROTE *THAT WAS THEN . . . THIS IS NOW* IN 1971; Emilio read it ten years later and was determined to make it into a movie. He actually completed the first draft before securing the rights to the property, so convinced was he that this would be his big-screen screenwriting debut.

By 1984, Emilio's option had run out and he still hadn't secured studio financing for the project. "The other Hinton novels' translations to film were disastrous," recalled Emilio, "and Hollywood was kind of Hinton-ed out."

Unable to come up with the two or three thousand dollars necessary to renew his option rights, Emilio found some financial backers in the Midwest to get involved with the project. "They had done a bunch of Chuck Norris films," said Emilio. "It made me a little gun-shy." But it was better than losing the project altogether. How many money-men put up major-league budgets for a twenty-two-year-old neophyte?

"They went through a couple of rewrites on it—the producers were acting as writers, and we all know what comes of a script when that happens. It was a bunch of forty-year-olds writing jokes for teenagers. Stupid. So I rewrote the script while I was doing *The Breakfast Club*. The producers hated it."

The picture looked like it might not get made until director Chris Cain entered the scene. He and Emilio churned out twenty pages of copy a day, sitting on the beach. They exchanged ideas, and then Emilio would go home and write down the dialogue.

The film finally went into production from mid-July to December of 1984 in the Minneapolis/St. Paul area. *That Was Then . . . This Is Now* is about the growing up, and growing apart, of two teenaged boys—raised as brothers—who help each other to survive the tough neighborhood in which they live. Emilio, as the younger brother, plays an alienated youth who is out to destroy himself. The film was finally released by Paramount in November of 1985.

Emilio could have had his name listed as associate producer on the project, but decided that "for my first time out, I didn't want too many credits." He stands listed only as star and screenwriter; nowhere in the credits does it hint that he personally gestated this project from the age of nineteen.

"It's taken me four-and-a-half years to finally get it to the screen," he said when the film was out. "It's been a lot of hard work; a lot of doors have been slammed in my face as far as studios are concerned. But to finally be sitting in that screening room and see 'Screenplay by Emilio Estevez' is overwhelming."

In another interview at the time, he elaborated, "During the selling of *That Was Then . . . This Is Now*, they thought, 'Oh, who is this punk, this little kid—he's trying to be a writer and an actor.' And at that point maybe it was a problem for them to see clearly, because I was not an established star. But it's a little easier for them to swallow now. I've got it made and I'm twenty-three years old, and that's proof enough at this point in my life.''

Film critic Leonard Maltin described the film in his book-length video guide: "Delinquent kid [Emilio], alienated from society, clings to his relationship with his adoptive brother [Craig Sheffer, in a role originally intended for Tom Cruise]—and freaks out when the older boy takes on a girlfriend [Kim Delaney], whom he sees as a threat.

"Estevez wrote the script from S.E. Hinton's young-adult novel, but its intense emotions probably read better than they play out on-screen. A variable film with some strong moments.''

That Was Then grossed $7.6 million in its first four weeks of release, more than repaying its backers and establishing Emilio as a potential money-maker in the movie industry. (One wonders if it would have earned more or less had the film retained the ending Emilio himself had wanted for it: a poignant shot of one of the friends left alone on the street.) Said Emilio, "Life is not this joyous thing all the time. And for films to portray make-believe happiness is silly.'' The existing ending— with Emilio's character landed in prison—isn't exactly upbeat, but it does mend the relationship between the two main characters.

That Was Then was a risky first-time screenwriting project for anyone, age notwithstanding and ending irregardless. "It's not a big picture, but it's big in emotional impact,'' said Emilio. "In it, I examine a very dark side that I think is in all of us, but our consciences keep it from surfacing. The dark side—that's the difference between going into McDonald's and ordering a hamburger and going into McDonald's and blasting everybody in the place: when people don't look into themselves, they have problems.''

Said Emilio, "I could have chosen to play the hero, the

guy who gets the girl. But when I read the book, I said, 'This is the guy I want to play,' so I tailor-made the character to me. I was able to infuse all my intensity and humor into one guy which I've never been able to do before.''

Having established himself as a power both behind and in front of the camera, Emilio went on to *St. Elmo's Fire*, a *Breakfast Club Goes to College* type of screenplay about a group of Ivy Leaguers starting their first year of "real life." Despite two number-one soundtrack songs, by John Parr and David Foster, the film was only moderately successful and took a critical drubbing.

Rob Lowe plays an irresponsible, hard-drinking musician who has seemingly forgotten his new wife and baby; Emilio portrays a bumbling but obsessively romantic law student who tracks his older-woman love interest through rain and snow, to no avail; Judd Nelson is cast as a promiscuous yuppie who thinks marrying Ally Sheedy will calm his libido and changing political parties will fatten his wallet; Andrew McCarthy plays a cynical scribe with writer's block and a fear of intimacy; Demi Moore emotes her throat out as a coked-up, debt-ridden party girl preoccupied with her not-yet-dead stepmother's funeral; Mare Winningham has the role of a rich, frumpy virgin who does welfare work and has a terminal crush on Lowe; and Ally Sheedy's character (the most level-headed of all) just wants to be friends with everyone and have an architectural career.

The whole project was less a movie than a class reunion. Rob Lowe had worked with Ally Sheedy on *Oxford Blues*, with Emilio on *The Outsiders*, and with Andrew McCarthy on *Class*. Judd Nelson and Sheedy worked with Emilio in *The Breakfast Club*. Daytime soaper Demi Moore was new to the group (although destined to have quite an impact), as was young film actress Mare Winningham.

But the fact that the cast was a bunch of buddies who

just happened to be actors ended up working against the film. As *Los Angeles Herald Examiner* critic Peter Rainer pointed out: "In principle, there's certainly nothing wrong with ensemble acting, and if it's between colleagues who are also cohorts, so much the better. After all, *St. Elmo's Fire* is about friendship. But with so many featured actors in the cast, the film never stops to take in any one of them for more than a few minutes in a stretch. . . . They're like a compendium of every coming-of-age cliché from every rites-of-passage movie in the last three decades. We can't understand why these friends are friends; the reason they must be together must be because—well, because they're the Brat Pack."

Chicago Tribune movie critic Gene Siskel was blunt: "Rarely has there been a group of more smug and obnoxious characters in a single film than in *St. Elmo's Fire*. . . . Jobs, marriage, sex, drug addiction—it's all too much for these bozos to handle." He also refers to the assemblage as "spoiled brat jerks . . . if director Joel Schumacher had only cut his cast in half and taken a more critical attitude towards the survivors, then *St. Elmo's Fire* might have worked as *The Breakfast Club* five years later. *St. Elmo's Fire* glorifies its kids' problems while trivializing their solutions."

In her *Glamour* magazine review, Charla Krupp felt that the problem wasn't so much the actors, but the roles they were given to play. It simply was not an accurate portrayal of the lifestyle it pretended to examine. "Yuppies don't hang out in bars," she insisted. "They don't drink heavily. They must be in control at all times. Yuppies aren't usually cocaine addicts. Cocaine is not a practical investment. Yuppies don't wreck cars and destroy homes. They probably respect possessions and real estate more than anything. . . . Though *St. Elmo's Fire* portrays yuppies as decadent, immoral brats who have no conscience, yuppies will probably flock to the movie. Yuppies are narcissists.

To see yourself slandered on screen is better than not seeing yourself at all.''

Almost without exception, the reviews of *St. Elmo's Fire* managed to work the word "brat" somewhere into the copy. Coincidentally, most of these very reviews appeared shortly after the *New York* magazine cover story that featured a shot of the *St. Elmo's* cast and coined the term Brat Pack—a sobriquet that has stuck like glue to Emilio (along with Lowe and Nelson and others).

It was during the auditions for *St. Elmo's Fire* that Emilio met Demi Moore; eventually, the two started dating. It was a gradual process. Said Moore in 1985, "We didn't have any scenes together in the film. But whenever the cast was photographed together, we just gravitated side by side.''

In the six months following *St. Elmo's Fire,* Emilio managed to complete three original screenplays. His output was becoming remarkably prolific. He has remembered sitting down in front of his portable computer at one time, with "a title: *Wisdom.* And I wanted to start with a guy sitting in a bathtub, reflecting on his life. That's all I had. Three weeks later, I had a first draft.''

Wisdom was to become Emilio's debut as a producer-director. But before he was able to secure financing for that project, he had a few other loose ends to tie up. For one, he narrated a social-service picture for Amber Lights, a warning to youngsters about the danger of drinking and driving. Then he was off to Wilmington, North Carolina during the summer of 1985 for work on *Maximum Overdrive.* This was the directorial debut for another prolific writer (and sometime actor), best-selling horror novelist Stephen King.

The story pits a small group of people at The Dixie Boy Truck Stop, a greasy spoon in the middle of nowhere, against a convoy of malevolent eighteen-wheelers that have somehow come alive—along with every other power machine in creation, from lawnmowers to circular saws. Emilio plays Bill Robinson, a parolee working as the diner's short-order cook and the eventual leader and hero of the trapped human survivors.

Stephen King admitted that Emilio was not really his first choice for the role. "I wanted Springsteen," he said with a laugh. Seriously, though, it was someone like Bruce Springsteen that he envisioned. "I needed a combination of working-class feel and box-office clout. I kept remembering Emilio from *Repo Man*, but I'd read the stories and didn't want any Hollywood bullshit."

After many discussions with the film's producers, casting agents, and managers, King went with Emilio for the role. "I was apprehensive," said King, "but ten minutes after we started working together, I knew that I'd made the right choice."

Now, King has said, "I wish I had *Maximum Overdrive* to do all over again. The only things right with that movie—and there weren't very many of them—I improvised. And Emilio knew that. He was a beginning-director's actor. He would do what you asked him to do. I got used to getting a lot of static from just about everyone except Emilio and Pat Hingle about my direction.

"I guess I wanted, at some point, to be a John Ford and say, 'You do it and you do it this way because I goddamn told you to do it this way.' With Pat, and especially Emilio, I didn't even have to think that way. If I had been like Oliver Stone and relaxed and just said, 'Go ahead, amaze me,' Emilio would have. But I didn't give him enough rope to free him up that way.

"Since I've always been an improvisational writer, I should have recognized Emilio's ability in that way. When I went into this, it was a whole new medium for me and I read about Hitchcock saying that for him the most interesting part of making a film was what went on before. The planning. Making the film itself was really sort of a bore. That's exactly what I wanted. I was scared to death of it.

So I did my sixteen hours of work a day before the film started. I came out with something that was like frozen in lucite. It was tough for people to move around. If I had it to do over again, I would loosen up a lot and the film would be better because of that.

"Emilio worked so damn hard. It was an education to watch him prepare," King noted. "If he was getting ready for a scene in which he was all pumped up, in a pressure situation, he'd come on the set and simply run around. Get really hot and get all the energy physically flowing. It was no big deal, no Method thing, no 'Get outta here, I'm getting ready to emote,' or any star-time shit. It was just matter-of-fact, 'I'm getting ready to go to work.' He has real good work habits and I respect that."

For Emilio, *Maximum Overdrive* was a welcome break in a string of dialogue-heavy movies he had done back-to-back. "The script landed on my desk and I said, 'Well, I'll give it a read,' " he recalled. "I'd been wanting to do an action picture for a while, and the script was wild. I saw that I'd get to shoot guns and grenade launchers, the whole thing. I could run, jump, be a hero, and get the girl. And I was broke," he added, practical to the end.

"Besides, when I was seventeen, I read *The Shining*, and had a lot of trouble sleeping afterwards. I've been a big fan of Stephen's work." Many filmgoers have been fans of King's work translated to film: *The Dead Zone* (featuring another member of this family), *Carrie, Cujo, Christine*—the list goes on and on, and some of the translations have worked. This time, however, the critics panned *Maximum Overdrive* as "stupid and boring."

But Emilio would have done it again, if only because it was during this project that he happened to meet British filmmaker Bernard Williams. Williams would become the producer of *Wisdom*, and Emilio wanted desperately to get his latest screenplay produced.

"I met Emilio in North Carolina while he was working

on *Maximum Overdrive*," Williams recalled a year later.
"I was producing *Manhunter* and we met at a party at
Dino's [de Laurentiis] house. He told me a bit about his
project, but when Gladden [Entertainment Corporation]
sent me a script several months later and asked me to take
a look at it as producer, I was amazed to discover it was
Emilio's screenplay for *Wisdom*."

▪ 12 ▪

A Little *Wisdom* . . .

EMILIO ESTEVEZ'S TRIAL-BY-FIRE IN THE FILM INDUSTRY WAS *Wisdom*, and he certainly gained a great deal of that during its genesis. Although the project was a commercial and critical failure, the fact that a twenty-three-year-old could have mounted his own production—as screenwriter, director, and lead actor—is startling in and of itself. Not only did he put a lot of himself into *Wisdom*, but there was a lot of himself in John Wisdom.

The official 20th Century Fox synopsis of the movie reads: "To some people, John Wisdom is a criminal; to some he's a hero; to others, he's just a man trying to revive the American Dream.

"Society hasn't left twenty-three-year-old John Wisdom many choices. Because of a youthful felony conviction for joyriding in a stolen car, all careers seem closed to him, from law clerk to fry cook. So he has invented his own job: He robs banks, but not for the money. And he does his job so well that he's wanted by the police in five different states.''

It's easy to see the many facets of himself that Emilio put into this character. For one, he has always nurtured a love-hate relationship with the spotlight, a spotlight that John Wisdom earns through his notoriety and Emilio earned through his birthright. He has seen many disputes with the law and with authority (particularly on the part of brother Charlie) and he has often felt that he is right and society is wrong. But still he harbors a great deal of respect for civilized behavior. There's a lot of ambivalence about an antihero who is in many ways a hero, as John Wisdom was intended to be. And this ambivalence was probably the single most defeating factor in his creation.

''I don't see John Wisdom as a role model,'' said Emilio. ''He is someone who starts off doing one thing, then gets caught up in being a national public figure. I wanted to make a statement about how crazed we are in this country with movie stars. It's almost a sickness, and I wanted to examine that: how easy it is to be exploited, which is what I think happens to this character. He ends up getting exploited.

''Throughout the film, while Wisdom and Karen are out on the road living their great adventure, we continually cut back to the parents, and the cop who's chasing him. The three of them are our anchors to reality, a way of saying: 'Excuse me, it's a very serious thing these two people are doing.' ''

In a later interview, Emilio also admitted, ''In a way, it's a very subversive film. A lot of people are angered by the message it gives the kids: If you want something changed, then pick up a gun and change it. But if they stay until the end, they'll realize that violence doesn't solve anything.''

Emilio's character is a strong-willed young man who cannot find a clear direction in his life. ''He's someone who got a raw deal because of that black mark by his name that prevents him from getting a job. He had great expectations of himself, and his parents had certain expectations of him, and life isn't going like he planned. So he reaches a point where he says, 'Society's left me no choice but to become the one thing I've really resisted becoming—a criminal.'

"But his conscience is too strong to be a criminal against the people, so he decides to become a criminal *for* the people."

The threads of fact and self-analysis that ran through *Wisdom* gave the screenplay a self-indulgent feel to many critics. Said *Entertainment Tonight* reporter Leonard Maltin, "Robert Wise assisted Estevez on the direction, which is certainly more competent than his wretched script; the film has one of the most self-defeating wrap-ups you'll ever see."

But those compliments about the direction should not be undervalued. After all, as the film publicist reminds us, "At age twenty-three, Emilio Estevez becomes the youngest member of the entertainment community to write, direct, and star in a major motion picture, joining a respected list that includes Orson Welles, Woody Allen, Charlie Chaplin, Alan Alda, Mel Brooks, and Sylvester Stallone." Certainly several of these experienced moviemakers have had a few bombs among them.

Author Stephen King also developed respect for Emilio's grasp of the craft. "He's a tremendously bright and ambitious young man. I mean that in all the best ways," said King. "Like a lot of people who are in the same situation and who get the shot, their reach sometimes exceeds their grasp at the start. And you get into a situation where you're hot and you're in a position where people are all very willing to give you all the rope you need to hang yourself.

"*Wisdom* had some great things in it. It had a great opening; a great come-out; and it had a great idea in the middle. I'm sure there are things that he would do differently if he had it to do over again. I'm interested in anything that he does.

"Based on that film and on *That Was Then . . . This Is Now*, I'd say that he's really an exceptional screenwriter," continued King. "That's not to say he's not an exceptional director. We live in an era right now—in movies as well as in books—there's a real blockbuster mentality. If you can't come out of the stall and make twenty to thirty million dollars on a film, your name is mud.

"I wish there were room—I wouldn't say exactly the old star system, although in a sense that's what I mean—some room for new people to be brought along and to fail in relative obscurity rather than on the cover of *People* magazine. To be the B-feature on a double bill, to learn your skills the same way Stanley Kubrick learned his. It's like trying to make movies or write books—be creative—in Dodger Stadium."

In many ways, *Wisdom* stands as a personal victory for Emilio. He not only brought the $6.5 million project in under budget by $200,000, but he wrapped the production one day ahead of schedule. Major miracles in themselves. And he won the respect and admiration of everyone around him.

"There's been tremendous cooperation from the crew," producer Bernard Williams said. "Emilio loves people. He shows it every day when he comes to the set and says, 'Hi, good morning.' He makes you feel good, and they respect him. They were pulling for him because they knew he had a tough job: *Wisdom* is an action movie with eighty locations and an eight-week schedule. That's a challenge for any director."

Another behind-the-scenes actor echoed Williams's plaudits. Mark Chilingar was Emilio's stand-in and photo double on the movie. (Since it was logistically impossible for Emilio to direct himself, he needed another actor to take his position in front of the cameras when he was behind them setting lineup shots.) "When I first met Emilio at his office at Lion's Gate, it was one of those situations where we both felt we had met before. I was impressed by his friendliness. He's easy to talk to, very approachable," said Chilingar.

"As a director, Emilio was extremely dedicated and every one of us involved liked working with him. He was very personable. Not that he was apt to go off with a couple of the guys for beers after completing the day's shoot; he had dailies from the previous day to screen, had to prepare for the following day's filming, and spent whatever quiet time he had with his girlfriend, Demi Moore, who was also in the film."

"There were times when he seemed a bit emotionally distant—no, preoccupied is really more accurate," continued Chilingar. "But with all the responsibilities he carried during this project, it was expected and no one thought less of him because he had a lot on his mind. He was intense in his commitment to the project. Every moment of his time, every bit of his energy, was taken up with work. In spite of all that was on his mind and his status on the project, he was always appreciative of the efforts of everyone around him. He was grateful, and we loved working with him. Regardless of how small the matter, he readily offered a sincere thank-you.

"I made some videos of people behind the scenes and Emilio would often be the biggest clown. He'd joke, he'd laugh. There were times when he'd take the video camera—it was actually his—and stalk around the set, jumping out at people from behind walls, or coming up from behind them. He was playing *Jaws* in his stalking." (That movie, by the way, is one of Emilio's favorites; he claims to have seen it more than seventy times.)

"There were times too, on the set," Chilingar noted, "when the atmosphere would get pretty intense over a scene or situation, but Emilio would manage to quickly bring things back into an easy equilibrium. He never made working difficult in any way.

"Occasionally, I think he let off any brewing steam of his own by being physical. He'd ride a bike around the area for a while, or if a group of extras was playing soccer, he'd spontaneously jump in and kick the ball around. And he always had enough energy to work out with weights during his short lunch break. He's very focused, yet easygoing and spontaneous, too."

Even when things were going wrong, as they will in any film, Emilio had a way of keeping the cast and crew at ease. "We were put behind schedule one day," Chilingar remembered, "because a cannon roll (a car stunt involving a car being rolled over after a high-speed chase) went wrong and had to be done again. There were a lot of people standing around waiting. Emilio made a point of riding his bike around, not only checking with the crew for progress reports, but to chat with the cast, to keep spirits up, and avoid having everyone get grumbly while we're sitting around not doing anything but waiting."

With fans and onlookers, "Emilio was pleasant, but had to keep things under control. There were masses of people watching the filming at times. He'd wave and smile, but he really couldn't take long periods of time to try to talk to them or sign a lot of autographs. That would have slowed things down; opened another can of worms."

Because *Wisdom* was such a monumental project for Emilio, it became a point of Sheen family focus. Both of his parents and each of his siblings made a point to visit the set several times during the two-month shoot.

Chilingar recalled: "Janet came by two or three times when I was on the set. And I particularly remember the day when Martin visited. The two of them came around, and I recognized him as he walked by. He's one of my all-time favorite actors, and of course I wanted to meet him. But I'm also sensitive about allowing people—especially someone like Martin who is constantly approached by strangers—their own room, their 'own space,' as is popular to say. That's truly how I feel, so I hung back. Eventually, he looked in my direction and just nodded. A little later, he walked over and held out his hand saying, 'Hi, my name is Martin.' He likes to get to know a little of the people around him. He's very outgoing, very friendly and warm.

"Janet is very quiet. Later, in Los Angeles, I met her again and was able to talk to her a bit. She's not overtly assertive, but she's approachable. It's very clear that her family is the number-one important focus in her life. She's very much a strong, healthy maternal influence. I think in somewhat large, busy families, it's often the mother who manages to pull everyone together, reminds individuals that they're part of a whole. She's a binding force."

Charlie had a cameo role in *Wisdom*; his video, *RPG*, was also incorporated into the script. Chilingar described the excitement around the set when Charlie was due to arrive. "Emilio was looking forward to seeing his brother. You could tell he was excited that Charlie was coming in from his work on *Platoon*. Actually, he had just completed the basic training part—the real-life boot-camp part—of his work on that film and had come in for just a few days of kind of R-and-R from the Philippines. He could have been concentrating on only having a good time while he was home, but he jumped into *Wisdom*.

"You could tell that the two brothers are tight. They have a lot of respect for each other. After their scenes together they spent the rest of the day together talking and catching up on things. It was obvious that they enjoyed each other's company."

Ramon, who was about to start work on the film *Turn Around*, also took time to stop by the *Wisdom* set before setting out for location. "Ramon was about to leave for

Oslo, Norway,'' said Chilingar. ''But he made certain to show his support for his brother's project, too. It's not as if it's an effort to do that in that family. They are all so close and supportive that it's just second nature to be aware of, and interested in, each other's work.

''Renee came up to Sacramento several times during the month we were filming there, too. Ramon is very proud of his sister, too, often reminding people how talented she is. Renee, like the rest of the family, is very easygoing and down-to-earth. I can't say enough nice things about them. I guess I'm really prejudiced, but they remind me of my family. We're all very close, too.''

Although he admits to a certain personal bias about *Wisdom*, Chilingar felt that the film had a lot of potential— much of it not realized. ''It's really a terrible shame that the final product wasn't as great as everyone involved had hoped. The final cut was not exactly all that great. There were a lot of things cut out of that film that were really very special. There were wonderful directorial moments, beautiful things with Veronica Cartwright and Tom Skerritt, that didn't make it to final print.''

One example that springs to Chilingar's mind is a final phone call made from John Wisdom to his mother, played by Cartwright. It was a scene the audience never got to see. ''The scene was a small set—supposed to be his mother's kitchen. The script woman, a few crew members, and I were watching Veronica in her scene. Every one of us started to cry, it was so moving. But it didn't make it to the final cut.''

Mistakes were made, but as brother Charlie noted, ''He went out and did it, and that's what's important. Never mind the critics . . . he had something, and he did something good. I was proud of him.''

Another bit of film never seen wasn't so much left on the cutting-room floor; rather, it was made an entirely different way because of *Wisdom*. Emilio was asked to star with Jane Alexander in the arty 1986 film *Square Dance*, but because he was still working on his own project, he turned it down. The role of the young retarded country boy went instead to old friend Rob Lowe.

Recalled Lowe, "Emilio called me and said, 'It's a great role, and I think you could really shine in it.' So I went over to his house and got the script, then called my manager and said I really wanted to play it. They couldn't understand why I wanted to do it . . . I did it for myself, to see if I could do it."

Brought up side by side, Rob and Emilio have seen both their careers and personal lives coexist in a Hollywood symbiosis. In one strange turn of fate, Rob found himself making love on-screen to the woman who was Emilio's love off-screen at the time: Demi Moore, in *About Last Night.* . . .

Lowe told a *Playgirl* magazine interviewer that he had talked it over with Emilio before doing the movie. "He was kind of uptight. . . . He said, 'Well, what if it was me and your girlfriend?' I said, 'I'd rather it be you than someone I didn't know.' He said, 'Yeah, yeah, that's true. I hadn't thought of that.' It's very difficult going out with anybody in this business, and this kind of thing is the first step to paying the price. It hasn't affected any of our relationships."

Passing up *Square Dance* gave Emilio the time to step into the film project that turned out to be his most commercial to date: *Stakeout*, with Richard Dreyfuss. More than one critic touted his performance and noted that he and veteran actor Dreyfuss made a terrific team, even if the story itself was improbable and, according to one scribe, "downright silly." Emilio (Bill) and Dreyfuss (Chris) are plain-clothes Seattle cops assigned to watch the house of a woman whose boyfriend has just escaped from prison. In disguise as a telephone repairman, Dreyfuss becomes the woman's lover, all the while knowing that his partner is spying on them. The movie combines an action-adventure cop plot with a romantic farce, and became a big hit of the summer of 1987.

"This is actually my first role playing an adult," commented Emilio. "A more mature, hardworking member of society." In his usual workaholic manner, Emilio went overboard to assure the authenticity of his character, studying the daily routine of undercover police firsthand. "I trained with the Crime Impact Team, a group of police officers who are members of the Sheriff's Department in Los Angeles County. I did ride-alongs, sat in on briefings, and participated in several stakeouts and high-speed pursuits. Seeing them in action and witnessing what they have to put up with, how they deal with people, gave me a much greater appreciation for police officers."

Emilio's performance in *Stakeout* caught the attention of an old acting buddy of his father's, Zooey Hall. "I've seen Emilio in a number of things, and in *Stakeout*, Emilio really established a great rapport with Richard Dreyfuss that made it one of the nicest things I've seen Richard do in a long time. And it's all Emilio doing this, not his father. He has his own talent. Of course, Martin raised a nice group of individuals!"

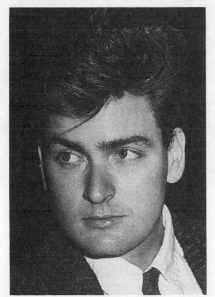

Named for (and pictured with) his father, Ramon, *top,* came late to acting. He was always the dancer in the family. 1982.

Carlos Estevez...as Charlie Sheen, the face of 1987, *left.*

Emilio at age 22 in 1984 participating in his favorite pastime: going to the movies, *above right.*

© PHOTOTEQUE

Martin Sheen relived the Vietnam War, *top,* in *Apocalypse Now.* A decade later, his son Charlie would do it again in *Platoon.*

Martin and Janet Sheen, *top right,* patriarch and matriarch of a remarkable clan.

Martin Sheen and his eldest, Emilio, *right middle,* at a Hollywood screening in 1987.

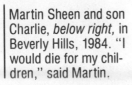

Martin Sheen and son Charlie, *below right,* in Beverly Hills, 1984. "I would die for my children," said Martin.

Andrew McCarthy, Emilio Estevez, Judd Nelson, and Rob Lowe as buddies who share the ups and downs of 'real' life after college graduation in *St. Elmo's Fire, top.*

Emilio Estevez and costar/former fiance Demi Moore, *above right,* in a publicity shot from *Wisdom.* 1986.

Brothers Emilio and Carlos Estevez, *bottom right,* inherited both their fraternal affection and cigarette habits.

© Phototeque

© Bob Scott/Star File

© PHOTOTEQUE

© ANDY SCHWARTZ/PHOTOTEQUE

© SMEAL/GALELLA, LTD.

© ANTHONY SAVIGNANO/GALELLA, LTD.

Platoon, left top, took ten years to get financed, and earned more than $130 million at the box office in one year.

Charlie spent summers as a teenager at baseball camp. *Opposite center,* he relives his childhood love at a Celebrity All-Star game at Dodger Stadium in 1986.

Does this look like a high school dropout? Charlie Sheen left during his senior year under a cloud, *left bottom.*

In *Wall Street,* Charlie Sheen, *top,* was reunited with director Oliver Stone and shared screen credit with his father.

© Photo Trends

© Ron Galella, Ltd.

Apocalpyse Now gave Martin Sheen his greatest starring role …and it almost killed him, *top*.

Martin Sheen in black tie in 1980, *left*. Martin has refused to participate in formal events that honor him.

▪ 13 ▪

Brat Pack Flack

IN THE SIXTIES, THE HOLLYWOOD HIERARCHY SEEMED RULED by a group of super-entertainers who dubbed themselves the Rat Pack: Frank Sinatra, Sammy Davis Jr., Dean Martin, Peter Lawford, and—honorarily—Shirley MacLaine. They drank together, partied together, and made movies together, and they were proud of their clubby appellation.

In 1985, *New York* magazine writer David Blum authored a cover story, originally intended as a piece about Emilio Estevez and *St. Elmo's Fire*, in which he dubbed a selection of the day's rising young stars as "Hollywood's Brat Pack." The phrase stuck, and opened up a can of worms for both the writer and the chosen young actors.

What made a Brat Packer? Its enrollees were all under twenty-five. They were hip, slick, and cool. They dressed in trendy clothes, including designer tee shirts. They found screen success almost overnight, having endured neither college matriculation nor years of acting school. They liked wine, women, and song. They liked one another.

The common sin of these usually well-heeled, often-second-generation industryites was that they had never paid any dues, by Blum's definition.

The cover story, which indicated that "everyone in Hollywood differs over who belongs in the Brat Pack," pinpointed Emilio, fresh from *St. Elmo's Fire*, as the "unofficial president" of the group. Other charter members included: Tom Cruise (whose credits at the time featured *The Outsiders*, *Taps*, and *Risky Business*); Rob Lowe (*The Outsiders*, *Class*, *The Hotel New Hampshire*, and *St. Elmo's Fire*); Judd Nelson (*Making the Grade*, *The Breakfast Club*, and *St. Elmo's Fire*); Timothy Hutton (*Ordinary People*, *Taps*, and *The Falcon and the Snowman*); Matt Dillon (*Tex*, *The Outsiders*, and *The Flamingo Kid*); Nicolas Cage (*Racing With the Moon*, *Birdy*); and Sean Penn (*Fast Times at Ridgemont High*, *The Falcon and The Snowman*, and *Racing With the Moon*).

The magazine feature seemed to scorn the young actors' affluence, carefree attitudes, and talents. It noted that Emilio, often willing to pick up the tab for his pals, went to some lengths to avoid paying for a six-dollar movie theater ticket. It disapproved of his easy success both in his career and with women; he earned a frown for having picked up a *Playboy* magazine centerfold model at the Hard Rock Cafe during a night out with the guys. Worst of all, Emilio seemed pleased to get into a nightclub ahead of the line of noncelebrity patrons.

The idea of being put into a clique is not in and of itself an affront to Emilio (or Charlie, who soon became an accepted Brat Packer, Jr.). After all, they named themselves the Point Dume Mafia when they and their friends and neighbors (ironically, friends and neighbors who are today full-fledged Brat Pack initiates) were out making their Super-8 extravaganzas. That self-styled group of hell-raising filmmakers included Emilio, Charlie, Sean and Chris Penn, Rob and Chad Lowe. But Emilio is bound and determined to separate himself from the clique that was picked for him: Never refer to him as a member of the Brat Pack within earshot. He calls that "a ridiculous label conjured up to try to sell magazines."

Supposed Brat Pack fellow Sean Penn—who has since graduated to the ranks of Hollywood's Bad Boys, up there with Robert Mitchum and Montgomery Clift—claimed that no such pack ever existed because, quite simply, as he said, "Ultimately, everyone is too much out for himself to be part of a real group." He also blasted the article that coined the phrase when he told *American Film* magazine, "All it is, is a condescending load of. . . . Sometimes writers, like actors—like anybody—do their work to impress three or four of their cool friends."

"I don't like being considered a part of a Brat Pack," Rob Lowe told movie critic Gene Shalit on the *Today* show. "It signifies that we're a group, but we're not." He simultaneously exemplified the title, however, by insisting on-air that "I learned to act on the big screen. I was never a spear carrier. I was always the star. Always."

Lowe continued to jostle the sleeping dog when he vented his anger at the Brat Pack label and the man who coined it in a *Chicago Sun-Times* interview: "David Blum burned a lot of bridges. He burned people early in their careers. He took on the wrong people, though. He's not Hunter Thompson or Tom Wolfe; he's David Blum living in a cheap flat."

The sad fact is that some members of the Pack will insist on proving the name appropriate. Sean Penn spent time in jail in 1987 for only the last in a long line of physical attacks on everyone from photographers to friends of his wife to, in this case, a movie extra. Even young Chad Lowe, Rob's baby brother, proved you don't have to be a Pack member to be a brat. He was rapped by NBC studio executives in early 1985 when, after taping six segments of their midseason sitcom entry, *Spencer*, he left the title role. ''Lowe's management people decided to build him up as a Broadway star and suddenly TV was beneath him. The network spokesperson added that part of the problem might have been that Lowe's best friend, Sean Penn, was a big movie star.

At the time, Chad was all of sixteen, a minor who required a guardian on the set. Sometimes big brother Rob, then twenty, would be the setsitter.

Now, Charlie Sheen ''became a junior member of the Brat Pack by association only,'' according to journalist Tom Green in a 1987 *Cosmopolitan* magazine article. But in the same article, Charlie himself rebutted, ''I've never been a Brat Packer and I've never been a teen idol and I'm very fortunate.'' Millions of young women would summarily refute the ''never have a teen idol'' part of that statement.

Chris Penn appears to be the only one of Emilio's childhood pals to have evaded the Pack pigeonhole. So far, he hasn't been accused of any brattish behavior in print, and even though he took up where his big brother left off in *Wild Life*, the sequel to *Fast Times at Ridgemont High*, he's managed not to be perceived as following in Sean's footsteps. ''I am Sean Penn's younger brother, but that doesn't mean I'll try to ride on his fame,'' he told *Newsweek* magazine. ''We're as close as two people can be, but we're also as different.''

The Brat Pack incident turned Emilio into an adamant antagonist of the press—especially the so-called celebrity press. But his wary attitude toward reporters had, in fact, been formed long before the *New York* magazine story had been written. His *Repo Man* costar, Sy Richardson, was quite impressed by Emilio's handling of journalists when the pair did a publicity tour for that film back in 1984: ''We were in Chicago one time,'' said Richardson, ''and about six guys from different newspapers and television stations were there interviewing him. Emilio would answer their questions to the point. He'd never give anything more; never take anything away. If they asked a question that only required a yes-or-no answer, that's all he gave them: yes or no.

"I questioned him about it," Richardson recalled. "And he said, 'Why? Because if I give them more than they want, they will take it and change it their way. If I give less, they will add on to it to make it make sense to them. So I listen very carefully and answer their questions to the point. This keeps you out of trouble.'"

After the Blum article, Emilio became vehement and vitriolic in his denunciation of liberties taken by the media. Blum, he felt, had personally betrayed him. "This writer came in from New York. He spent like three days with me, questioning me, we talked about all kinds of things, we got into a lot of areas. I took him out with the guys one night and that's all he wrote about—this night out with the guys—from a very catty point of view. He made us sound like a bunch of arrogant pricks!

"Sean wasn't there—but this guy made a lot of digs at all of us which has made me a little guarded around the press," he understated. "Another thing this article tried to point out is that we are a bunch of backstabbers; that we are very competitive amongst ourselves. It's just the opposite. We are very, very supportive of each other, extremely supportive.

"If Sean sees me in a picture, he'll call me up from the theater and say, 'Hey, man, I've just seen your movie.' I saw *Falcon and the Snowman* and he was brilliant. I called him up and said, 'Hey Sean, you're happening!' We are strangely uncompetitive." (This is obviously a topic that the don't-call-them-Brat-Packers haven't discussed together at length!)

A few weeks after making the above comments, Emilio was still hot under the collar about the Blum article. He voiced his anger in yet another interview: "It had started out as a profile of me and turned into a young-actors piece, so a lot of us were lied to. Until two weeks before it went on the stands, they still maintained that it was a profile of me. You know, you've got to laugh about it. It was silly. The writer's jealousy came out—more than anything else his jealousy really came out. He did a hatchet job on us, that's what he did. He was privy to something that I guess every young writer would want to be privy to, but he abused the privilege.

"As a result," he went on to tell *Film Journal* reporter Elizabeth Gordon, "all journalists that want to talk to these young actors are going to suffer from this one guy. . . . You'll only know about me professionally and that's it. I'm not willing to share myself on a personal level with any journalists, probably for the rest of my life, because I've been burned so badly."

How has the man who started this whole brouhaha, David Blum, reacted to the furor he unleashed? Mostly, he stands his ground. Two years after the original story appeared, he found himself bylining a piece in the *Los Angeles Times* Sunday magazine entitled, "The Brat Pack Strikes Back: Why One Writer is Weary of His Words." He explained: "The whole thing began as a profile of a nice guy named Emilio Estevez, and it would have stayed that way were it not for two things. First, he insisted on getting a free pass to . . . a movie, when tickets only cost six dollars. I thought that was a bratty thing to do. Second, he kept telling me about all of his movie-star friends and how they liked to hang out together, drink beers, party hearty—that sort of thing. He offered to take me out with them for a night on the town and I accepted."

Blum partied hearty that night with Emilio, Rob Lowe, Judd Nelson, and Jay McInerney (author of *Bright Lights, Big City,* later a film vehicle for another young actor, Michael J. Fox). They hung out until the wee hours of the morning. The next day, still recovering from a hangover as he drove along Sunset Boulevard, Blum remembered a journalist-friend referring to himself as a member of the "Fat Pack" after going from restaurant to restaurant on assignment. "Suddenly the phrase 'Brat Pack' came to mind," said Blum. "I wouldn't call it inspiration exactly. I did think it was pretty clever."

Blum felt it was a reasonably accurate description, along with a smart turn of phrase. Even though these were people he had "gotten to know ever so slightly through my reporting, they had been acting like . . . brats. Which is not to say that I would not have acted precisely the same way if I were twenty-three years old, famous, and rich," Blum admitted. "But these guys definitely fit the bill. They would disagree with my assessment, but the fact is, I do have one thing they don't. A job at a magazine. And that entitles me to the freedom of the press."

Not all other members of the literary estate were to uphold Blum's rights in this matter. He was, he remembered, a bit shocked at the response of *Time* magazine critic Richard Schickel, who publicly blasted him on the *Donahue* show (along with some guest actors on the podium). Schickel said, "I really thought that was a scurrilous article . . . I really think this is a kind of scuzz journalism . . . ." and offered to apologize to the actors on behalf of his profession.

Blum pointed out, "Schickel was referring to the fact that I had supposedly told the gang of actors at the Hard Rock Cafe that everything would be off the record. That isn't true."

Schickel's critical colleague, Gene Siskel of the *Chicago Tribune*, is a bit more sympathetic to Blum's original manuscript: "The article was well-written. Beyond looking at those individuals named in the article, I think the value of that article—beyond the sloganeering—was the question it raised. How well-trained are these young people who are making big sums of money to star in pictures? That's a very valid question.

"Look who came to stardom in 1987, just two years later—Dennis Quaid, who is thirty-three; Kevin Costner, who is thirty-two. These men have put in some time. Quaid told me that the reason he feels he's not likely to blow up under the pressure of his newfound success is that he is relatively older than some of these younger actors who had trouble adjusting. I believe that's probably true. There's a lot of seasoning that has gone on. With some—not all—of those younger actors, a sort of cult sprung up around some with less experience than we're used to. I'm sure a lot about the business, including the press, shook them up."

And, Siskel noted, Emilio didn't really do a bad job in defending himself against the accusations of the article at the time. "A lot of kids got a real smack in the face with that article. And at the time, Emilio had to deal with that subject."

Today, David Blum—who makes a point to define himself as "a reporter, not a critic"—says of celebrity interviews: "Generally, the journalist-actor relationship serves two purposes. The actor is seeking publicity; the journalist tries to get as much time and insight into that person as he can so he can write an informed article. It's a calculated tradeoff."

Back in 1985, Emilio believed the interview that Blum was going to write would focus only on him. Blum agreed that was his original intention: "I originally set out to do it that way, on Emilio only. He graciously allowed me a lot of access to him and a lot of his friends. I decided that, at the end of my reporting, I had a story far more interesting than the one I had initially set out to do. I felt it was far more appropriate to write that story than merely the interview. That's what I did, and I still feel it was an appropriate decision. Obviously, some people do not."

As to the reaction his famous feature evoked, Blum said, "Because they are in a position to reach far more people than I can, perhaps they ultimately had the advantage. But I'm glad they had the opportunity to speak out. That's what the press offers. It's been an interesting dialogue!''

Blum continued, ''Is a journalist bound to report the story he was sent to get, or report what is, in fact, the story as it reveals itself? I believe it's a journalist's responsibility to provide the latter. Otherwise, reporters are merely delivering the preconceived notions and theories developed by editors and press agents. I am a reporter of my observations. And that's what I did, and continue to do. At the time of the Hollywood Brat Pack feature, I reported about a specific group of actors who I specifically named at a specific point in time. Unfortunately, I happened to coin a phrase that has come to mean any number of endless things over which I have no control.''

In a *Vanity Fair* magazine interview with Sean Penn, writer James Walcott noted, ''It's remarkable how thick the movies are now with blood brothers . . . acting has become a guild for male hormones and bonding rituals.'' He also noted that Penn is close friends with Emilio, and Timothy Hutton. The term Brat Pack is used without definition; it no longer needs one.

During the production of *The Breakfast Club*, costar Paul Gleason remembered, ''I know he doesn't like the label of being a member of a Brat Pack, and he's certainly as far from any brat as you can get. But, one day he said I was an honorary member of the Brat Pack. I take that as a compliment!''

Stephen King recalled his work with Emilio on *Maximum Overdrive* and defended him: ''We ain't seen nothing from the kid yet. The kid's going to be big. Really big. I still call him the kid. Well, he don't act like no kid, or think like one neither. You know all this Brat Pack bullshit? I'll tell you, I'd pay a million bucks for each of my kids if I could be guaranteed they'd turn out like Emilio.''

With the issue of Brat Pack aside, the press continues to be a mystery—and worse—to Emilio. He'll never forget a luncheon date with Gene Siskel. Emilio said, "Five minutes into lunch, he [Siskel] says, 'Estevez, the press is not your friend.' I lost my appetite. I don't know why people want to put out such bad energy. It's not the way I choose to relate to the human race."

Gene Siskel remembered the 1986 interview in Emilio's Chicago hotel suite, but was unaware of Emilio's later comment about it. When reminded of his own remark about the press, Siskel acknowledged, "I would say that to just about anyone. At the time, I was talking as a forty-one-year-old journalist to a twenty-three or twenty-four-year-old actor. I was reminding him not to be naive about the press.

"As a member of the press for nineteen years, I don't see my role as the actor's 'friend.' That's just the way things are," observed Siskel. "I've written movie reviews, interviews, trend stories. I'm always functioning as a critic, be it in an interview, movie review, or even as the subject of an interview. A reporter reports, as objectively as possible; a critic offers an opinion. Friendship is irrelevant. There's not an actor who is a 'friend' of mine. When I get sick, they don't call. A friend would.

"When it's functioning well, the press is trying to accurately describe what went on. In the case of the performing arts, criticism—ideally—is the expression of one's opinion in an effort to, possibly, better the medium. That's not to say that if the press is not a friend, it is, per se, an enemy."

Siskel actually is fairly positive about Emilio personally, and remembered being glad that he "has never done a sequel. I like a lot of the work Emilio has done. I think that proves he's an actor into his profession for more than the money. He wants to do a good job."

Emilio is not the only family member Siskel has interviewed. He did a lengthy interview with Martin. "He's very thoughtful; a fine, great actor. Dealt with the issues raised and answered the questions honestly and not always in his favor. I found him to be always interesting; almost as interesting off-screen as on, and that's a compliment to him.''

Emilio's avoidance of the press is not based on a thin-skin sensitivity towards professional criticism. Clearly, he feels there are simply areas of an actor's life that should remain private even when the individual has chosen a public position for his career. In 1985 when Emilio was hit with a paternity suit, an inquiring columnist was told by Emilio's press representative that she ''was not free to comment on the situation.'' To Emilio, it was simply no one's business but his own. (Charlie carried the idea one step further, when he actually called a gossip columnist at her home—at 6 A.M.!—to dispute the facts of an item that had run in the press linking him with actress Daryl Hannah. Not only was it no one's business but it wasn't true, and he wanted to know where she got the information.)

Another time, during his romance with actress Demi Moore, Emilio found himself grudgingly admitting, ''I don't really want the press to know about us, but they do—and I'm not ashamed. I love her.''

Still another reporter raised his ire when she called to do a fact verification that his relationship with Moore ''blows hot and cold.'' At the time he told the reporter that ''she [Demi] is the love of my life and always has been. So they put it as on-again-off-again. . . . I lead a very private life in L.A. ever since that article.''

His desire for privacy also led him to invest a portion of his film earnings in a chunk of secluded Montana real estate, which will have the added advantage of giving him private slopes for his favorite hobby, skiing.

▪ 14 ▪

The Loves of His Life

WHILE THE BRAT PACK HAS A REPUTATION FOR LOVING 'EM and leaving 'em—and both Charlie and Emilio have been seen dating (or voiced the desire to date) some of the most beautiful women that ever graced the cover of a magazine—the fact is that Emilio has always tended more towards his father's singleminded monogamy. Emilio is more *serially* monogamous, however, and his definition of monogamy doesn't always include matrimony.

One of Emilio's first loves was a Wilhelmena model, Carey Salley, whom he dated for more than three years, starting before he was twenty years old. She was long and lithe with a mane of dark brown hair. They had their pictures taken together and displayed in *People* magazine; they were inseparable. He spoke publicly of his love for her. He had two children with her.

Then, at the auditions of *St. Elmo's Fire*, he met sultry-voiced, smoldery-eyed actress Demi Moore. And it was Demi who almost got him to the altar.

By August of 1985, a Hollywood trade publication had noted that "youngsters Demi Moore and Emilio Estevez are 'kinda engaged,' which means they won't set a date for some time." A few weeks later, a date was not exactly set, but a time frame was established.

According to a friend of Demi and associate of the Sheen family, "I remember running into them at Helena's [a private dinner club in Los Angeles] one night, just a few months after they had met. They were glowing. Demi was so excited and everything was going just great in Demi's life. They were in love and already talking about marriage, looking at houses. The wedding was going to be around Christmas of the following year."

The couple told real-estate magnate Jim Fox that they wanted to use his beachfront mansion as the site for the nuptials; invitations were set for printing and stated December 7, 1986 as the wedding date.

However, in the next fifteen months, although Emilio had insisted several times to the press that Demi was the love of his life, a lot happened. For Demi, *One Crazy Summer* and *About Last Night* . . . happened, propelling her into major star status. For Emilio, *That Was Then . . . This Is Now* and *Maximum Overdrive* happened; and, for both of them, *Wisdom*. That's a lot of work, pressure, and stress for a little over a year, and particular pressure when the pair is working together on one movie.

But the relationship survived all that. What it did not seem able to survive was the reemergence of Carey Salley.

In the autumn of 1985, celebrity attorney Marvin Mitchelson served Emilio with a $3 million paternity suit that also asked $15,000-per-month child support (in lieu of the much smaller amount Emilio had already been paying for the previous sixteen months) for his client, Carey Salley, whose son Taylor Levi Salley had been born on June 22, 1984. The suit also included stipulations regarding the child Carey was then expecting, and later delivered: a daughter, Paloma Estevez, on February 18, 1986.

Mitchelson told a Hollywood columnist that Emilio and Carey "lived together on and off for four years; he left her for Demi Moore, is my understanding. . . . Estevez is not denying paternity of Carey's baby or the child she's expecting—but we've filed a petition to establish paternity officially."

According to one of Demi's girlfriends, "It wasn't even so much the children that added to the problems in the eventual breakup between Demi and Emilio . . . not of themselves.

"Emilio had to spend a lot of time with his kids and Demi really didn't want a ready-made family, especially with the children's mother so prominently still in the family, too. All the kids—including Charlie's little daughter, including their mothers—all get together around the holidays. Christmas is a real big deal at the Sheen household."

As the date for the wedding got closer, the holiday atmosphere around the homestead "reminded Demi of the year before," said her friend. "Everyone had been together and there was Carey with one baby in her arms and another on the way. This year they'd all be together again . . . and she realized she'd have to live with that situation on every holiday for all the years to come. The bottom line was that she didn't want to deal with that.

"The invitations were out and gifts had started to arrive. But the packages were returned and the wedding was cancelled. Demi and Emilio had been living together for quite some time by then, and had even bought a house together on the beach about a year before."

Yet the couple did not totally scrap the marriage plans for several months. In fact, they shrugged off the "postponement" of the arrangements as being due to their conflicting career schedules. He had commitments to postproduction work for *Wisdom*, and Demi was involved in a stage role in

New York at the time. Later, in a January of 1987 interview, Emilio told reporter Diana Haithman, "We're both kind of strung out, and we want our wedding to be special. Even if we elope, we want it to be a special day, not just squeezed in."

This was to have been Emilio's first marriage, of course, but such was not the case with Demi. As a teenager, she lived for two years with rock musician Freddy Moore, and married him when she was nineteen. They met when she attended a concert by his pop-rock band, Boy. She wrote songs with Freddy and they appeared in the low-budget movie, *Parasites,* together. Their marriage lasted almost two years and they divorced while she had a leading role on television's daytime soap opera *General Hospital.*

Being all too aware of Emilio's past was one reason that Demi broke up with him in the spring of 1987. But it's possible that Emilio never even knew about Freddy; when Demi married television star Bruce Willis after a whirlwind romance in 1987—only a few months after the final split with Emilio—she declared on her application for a marriage license that it was her first marriage. She became Mrs. Bruce Willis in a Las Vegas hotel suite on November 22. Mrs. Freddy Moore became banished from memory.

In the ensuing months, Emilio kept a low romantic profile. Lately, however, he's been linked with several ladies, including model Marla Hansen, who made headlines several years ago when she became the victim of a razor-wielding attacker in New York. But friends and associates insist that "he's just dating and is definitely not involved with any one lady."

Wife and family, though, are definitely in Emilio's future plans. He told a reporter in a 1985 interview that "I'll have at least four kids." With half his goal already reached, he has made a good start!

· 15 ·

Charlie, Dear Charlie

CARLOS IRWIN ESTEVEZ WAS BORN ON SEPTEMBER 3, 1965—
and it wasn't an easy birth. "He came into the world
screaming," recalled his father some twenty-two years
later, "and hasn't stopped since."

In the beginning, Charlie vented that energy in both
typical and not-so-typical boyhood pursuits: Before he completed his first decade of life, Charlie was familiar not only
with sandlot ball, but also movie sets, cameras, and scripts.
He was only five when big brother Emilio enlisted his
nascent talents in the neighborhood kids' Super-8 productions. Of course, the neighborhood kids at Point Dume
(near Malibu) included such soon-to-be-stellar names as
Sean and Chris Penn, Chad and Rob Lowe . . . some
neighborhood!

The boys played out many of the usual mysteries and
shoot-'em-ups (plenty of those!) that rambunctious hellraisers
of their age are drawn to. But they proved that a little
knowledge can be a dangerous thing, or at least an expen-

sive one. Pointing a thumb-and-index-finger gun while yelling "Bang! Bang! You're dead!" would have satisfied most other make-believe hooligans; this troupe, however, knew the tricks of the trade. Prop-department handguns that fired blank ammunition and realistic blood packets were a must. Production costs on each of the boys' movies would run as high as $100. Luckily, when their allowances ran out, someone in the gang could usually sweet-talk a parent into becoming a funding "executive producer."

Charlie's favorite one-reeler is titled *Street Kids*, a *filmette noir* in which Sean Penn, playing a murderous drug dealer, eventually gets thrown off a cliff. "I grew up on movie sets," said Charlie, "and was a Super-8 filmmaker since I was five. I wrote, directed, produced, and acted in these shorts along with the others in the Point Dume Mafia. I've always needed to have an outlet for some form of creative expression in my life."

He was only seven when he joined his father on location for *Badlands*. Summer vacations and family holidays were filled not only with aunts, uncles, barbeques, and amusement parks, but with cameras and celebrities. Traveling to his father's film locations took Charlie and the rest of the clan from Hong Kong to Switzerland and almost everywhere in between. Sometimes the jaunts would fall within a school vacation period; when they did not, tutors would fill the educational gap.

"I didn't really care," said Charlie of his haphazard scholastic foundation. "I learned more in one day on a movie set than I ever did in any semester in school."

At nine years of age, Charlie made his professional acting debut in his father's acclaimed television drama, *The Execution of Private Slovik*. He was an extra in the wedding scene. Not a big part; at the time, not even a part that swayed his primary interest from sports to acting.

Charlie spent about ten months in the Philippines during the filming of *Apocalypse Now*, and the company of Marlon

Brando, Robert Duvall, and Francis Ford Coppola further piqued his curiosity in this star business. Of course, the family's turmoil over Martin's illness overshadowed all else. Still, a walk-on part in that blockbuster was nearly as glamorous as becoming a baseball star to the twelve-year-old.

"I guess that's when I decided I should give acting a shot," said Charlie. "Being exposed to that environment at that age made me realize that there's more to life than baseball."

During Charlie's high school years, though, his focus was athletic, never academic or even theatrical. At Santa Monica High School he played basketball, football, and golf, but became most agile on the baseball diamond. Whenever possible, he spent his summers at the Mickey Owen Baseball School near Miller, Missouri and later said, "If I weren't an actor, I'd be playing college baseball right now.

"During high school, I wanted to be a baseball player because nobody else in the family played baseball. Emilio wrestled and played soccer. I thought that if I could excel at baseball, they'll think I'm something. *I'll* think I'm something. I loved baseball."

With professional success to bolster him, Charlie has no problem (if he ever did) admitting that he never really took his high school studies seriously. "My attendance record ran about thirty percent," he has boasted more than once. "Three-day weekends were mandatory. The last book I took home was midway through my sophomore year.

"But I never missed baseball practice, because I was the next Cincinnati shortstop," he said in a 1986 interview.

His long weekends began in earnest when he turned sixteen, and his parents presented him with his first car. ("The beginning of my demise," he admitted to a *Cosmopolitan* reporter.) It was a BMW—or "Beemer," as the local vernacular has it. He most often drove it to Westwood, the UCLA "college town" in western Los

Angeles, filled with movie theaters, cute bistros, fast-food shacks, bookstores, and plenty of pretty coeds.

"Westwood was my high school career," said Charlie. "I call it my stomping ground." With the freedom of wheels, Charlie found life in the fast lane more fun than last row in biology or English class (those were the subjects he usually failed). Shortly after getting his car, Charlie was arrested for the first—but not the last—time.

It was after a particularly taxing party night that the Malibu sheriffs discovered young Charlie passed out over his steering wheel in the middle of a Pacific Coast Highway intersection. Rubbing salt in the official wound was a small knife strapped to this comatose minor's ankle, and a customized baseball bat in the car that the officer felt was intended for banging something other than horsehide.

Six years after the incident, Charlie's dad commented in a *Vanity Fair* interview, "If he'd been black, he'd still be in jail." Martin excused the knife by noting that during his son's time on the *Apocalypse* set, "He got very fond of weapons." Nor does dad think his sloe-eyed boy is any danger to society: "He's got the world's biggest heart, but he's got a lot of anger."

Summertimes are hot in Southern California for a boy with a flashpoint temper, and high school didn't offer baseball over the holidays; the Sheen parents decided that sending Charlie to baseball camp, *without* a car, sounded like a pretty good idea. The young sportsman enjoyed it for three or four seasons, even though it meant leaving the town of Westwood behind. Leaving the girls of Westwood behind was another matter, and one that took its toll at camp.

Ken Rizzo, the owner and administrator of the Mickey Owen baseball program, was the camp director at the time of Charlie's summertime visits. "Charlie definitely had athletic talent for baseball," said Rizzo. "He was a very good offensive player. It was clear that he had interest in pursuing baseball beyond high school athletics.

"I remember several times when we'd sit on the porch and he'd want to know about his prospects. He was concerned about being a good shortstop in particular. He was serious about the sport, and about taking a good look at his abilities. And he was very intense, very vocal, when he was playing."

The school is set in the rural environment of the Ozark Mountains. Eight to ten young athletes and a counselor slept in each rustic cabin. The ballplayers-to-be were expected to keep their cabin area neat, get their laundry done, have meals at specific times—and study, play, and enjoy baseball for the rest of the day. Sessions were two weeks long.

A typical day for the boys of summer started with a 7:30 A.M. reveille and breakfast at picnic tables in the mess hall. From 9:30 to 11:30, they worked with coaches and instructors on one of the six baseball fields or in a classroom. Lunch was 11:30 to 12:30.

Early afternoons were devoted to batting practice or customized workouts, and by 2 P.M. everyone was back on the playing field for intense practice. Field work continued until 4:30, dinner ran until 6, and then it was back out on the field for night games until 10 o'clock. Lights-out was at 10:30 sharp, with no exceptions.

The only resemblance Mickey Owen bore to Charlie's Malibu lifestyle was that all the games were videotaped. And you can be sure that at least one camper had his eyes on the camera angles as carefully as he did on the ball.

One would think that Charlie was destined to be the camp's foremost disciplinary case, but Rizzo remembered him with affection—even if he did almost have to expel him at one time. "He's not one to be comfortable with any rigid authority, that was clear," said Rizzo. "But he wasn't rebellious. Charlie blended in well with the other fellows.

"I remember that on the first day, Martin and Emilio came down with Charlie," Rizzo said. "Martin always kind of looks the same, but Emilio—well, he was sure different than he is now. When I saw him on the movie screen years later, it was like another person. He had been so slight and gangly during high school. Charlie looks more mature now, more manly, of course.

"Charlie was a rather quiet kid, a very nice kid," Rizzo recalled. "He really wasn't shy though; more introspective and laid back. You could see the thoughts at work behind his eyes. Nothing was done out of the ordinary for him because of his father. Nothing more was expected of him either. But I think he expected more from himself all the time. It was important for him to achieve certain self-created goals. That's admirable.

"I doubt that most realized who he was, or really cared. The boys were all myopic about baseball. That was their only real interest while at camp."

Considering Charlie's antics in high school, it would be hard to imagine his baseball-camp interlude passing without incident. Nor did it. Rizzo thought that the rural environment of the camp must have taken Charlie some effort to get used to. "After all, he was from Malibu. He grew up in a pretty stimulating atmosphere," Rizzo said, noting also that, compared to Charlie's travels to his dad's movie locations, the Mickey Owen Baseball School paled by comparison.

So Rizzo may have allowed the obstreperous Sheen a margin of tolerance when Charlie took an unannounced and unauthorized trek to a general store about half a mile down the road where he managed to get a ride into town. "Well, none of the boys was supposed to do that," Rizzo said. "But Charlie comes from a different background . . . I'm certain he wasn't being malicious.

"But we had to lean on him pretty heavily for leaving. After all, we're responsible. But he had just gotten a little bored with the routine. Wanted to get out on his own. He left in the afternoon and came back very late that night

. . . about two o'clock in the morning. We were up waiting for him. A local girl with several of her girlfriends in the car drove him back.

"We told him that anyone who leaves the camp like that has to be sent home. And he really didn't want to do that. He wanted to finish the session so badly he was nearly in tears. I wasn't as hard on him as the assistant director at the time was. . . . Charlie got the idea; toed the line completely after that, and he came back other summers. I made the decision to let him stay. Heck, I remember being sixteen and seventeen, too. Every male has to sow his oats.''

Back in Malibu, Charlie immediately hopped back into his beloved car. After all, it was also the way Charlie got himself to the smattering of acting auditions that came his way. When he was seventeen and in his junior year, he auditioned for a feature film, *Grizzly II: The Predator*, but it would be over a year before he found out he had landed the costarring role in that project. And, as fate would have it, that delay actually proved to be perfect timing: There was enough drama going on in the restless teen's life for the next fourteen months.

Charlie's school grades, which during his first year and a half showed a healthy dose of A's (in graphics, physical education, history, wood projects, and algebra), B's (typing, English, Spanish, and geography), and C's (drama, machine shop), slipped to D's (driver education, design) and failures by mid-1983.

"I just kept sliding by,'' Charlie admitted. "I hustled my way out of F's with makeup work to get D's, so I could still play baseball. I had a really good arm for somebody my build.'' He had grown to five feet, ten inches and 150 pounds. "Shortstop size,'' Charlie called it.

In his senior year, with a cumulative grade point average of 1.35 and ranking 778 in a class of 793, Carlos Estevez—as he still called himself—withdrew without earning his diploma. This, in spite of earning a baseball scholarship to the University of Kansas.

Actually, there was a little more to the story than below-average grades and spotty attendance. There was also the matter of an arrest for credit-card fraud during his senior year. "It was curiosity, boredom, aversion, sudden profit," Charlie explained in a 1986 newspaper interview in Chicago. "There was no gun at my head. My buddy showed me the things he had heisted. I saw no flaws. I did it. My 'crime spree' lasted a week.

"My friend found some credit-card receipts in a wastebasket. It made perfect sense to both of us to call up and order a couple of portable TVs," he confessed. "As I told a high-class Beverly Hills lawyer who got me off, it was an identity thing. I had some time to think about it while I was in the cell for fifteen hours. I've thought about it since then, too. I don't regret it. You can't live with regrets.

"Besides, now, as an actor, I can relate to the criminal mind," said the hereditary thespian.

The final curtain in Charlie's high school drama fell on the last day of class. Charlie called it "the episode that led to my acting career, when I threatened the life of my English teacher."

He explained: "I needed a C to graduate. She wouldn't let me take the final because I didn't have the readmit, the slip readmitting me to the classroom. I crumpled up the exam paper and threw it in her face and left." He did offer a slightly harder version to David Letterman, saying "Okay, so I threw a desk and a trash can. It was very dramatic. Actually, it was my first good performance!" (The teacher, apparently, was so convinced by his "performance" that she filed a complaint with the police, claiming Charlie had threatened her life.)

Still, Charlie could have eaten humble pie and probably gotten his diploma. But humble pie is hardly his favorite meal, and he had one last bit of adolescent acting-out to do before closing the door on his high school career—with a slam-bang. It was the day his high school baseball team was scheduled in the national semifinals against the number-one team in California. . . .

"I was either going to pitch or play shortstop," recalled Charlie. "It was to be the biggest game of my life—but then the dean called me in and said I was off the team." Charlie had failed English, an automatic exclusion; he took his case to the principal, and there was a final confrontation.

"I didn't even get my first word out before he said, 'There's no way you're going to put a uniform on,' and I was blown away! Leaving the building I was in such a rage that I picked up a rock," said Charlie. "I figured, 'It's the last day, let's take out a window!' I threw it at high speed; I let it fly. There was only one open window on the entire face of the building, and the rock went right through it.

"So I figured, if I can't even break a window in this place, I'm out of here. That was my last day in high school."

Without taking the English exam, there was no possibility that Charlie could earn the necessary C for graduation. The baseball scholarship was worthless without a high school diploma; Charlie had no real alternative but to try his luck in acting.

Now came the hard part—telling his parents. Charlie said, "My parents knew that eventually I'd go on to bigger and better things. They trusted my character. But they were disappointed when I quit high school without graduating. I'd always say to Dad, 'Well, Dad, you know what happened to you. You were eighteen, didn't graduate, jumped on a bus to New York with Al Pacino. C'mon, talk to me.' "

"Charlie was always talking about baseball," remembered Cara Poston, another Santa Monica High School student at the time. "Baseball, baseball, baseball. No one ever figured that he'd ever become an actor. That was Emilio's department.

"And, Charlie was always just a little skinny kid. Now he's a hunked-up, sex-symbol movie star! But back in high school, Charlie was only interested in baseball. He was a nice guy, but no one guessed he'd be a celebrity like he is today."

Neither did Charlie.

▪ 16 ▪

Lights, Cameras, More Action

LESS THAN THREE MONTHS AFTER WITHDRAWING FROM SANTA Monica High School, Carlos Estevez landed his first feature-film role, and officially took the name Charlie Sheen. It never worried him that people would draw comparisons to his famous and well-respected father: "I'm his biggest fan," Charlie has said of his dad. "I have so much respect for him I couldn't possibly find the words to express it. I have more of a brotherly relationship with him than a father-son relationship."

"It would be an understatement to say that I have been influenced by my father acting-wise," Charlie told *Hollywood Reporter* magazine editor Leonora Langley. "He's the only guy I listen to. When it comes to understanding characterization or interpretation of a role, a scene, a line, or a moment, he's the best actor alive."

And, given Charlie's past experience with the academic world, he felt a definite sympathy with Martin's views and advice about acting . . . and acting school. "Dad told me,

'Don't become a classroom actor. Don't go out and do it by the book. Work with me and learn in front of the camera.'

"When I was going to my first job, I was kind of nervous," Charlie admitted on several occasions. "Dad said, 'Just don't tell any lies. Make the camera your best friend, but ignore it at the same time.' And he said that we are the commodity in this business and this town loves talent. He said, 'Always remember that, because they're going to try to suck you dry.' This is before I'd done one film!

"I said, 'Dad, how do you know I'm going to work after this?' And he said, 'I just know. I see it in your eyes.' He said, 'Just be true to yourself.' "

With his official, Screen Actors Guild-approved name and lots of enthusiasm, Charlie was off on a three-week shoot in eastern Europe to make *Grizzly II: The Predator*, in which he costarred with Louise Fletcher and Laura Dern (another second-generation Hollywoodite, daughter of Bruce Dern). The film was originally scheduled for release in December of 1984, and to date has still never made it to theaters. (With Charlie's newfound celebrity status, however, filmmakers can expect a profitable video-cassette.) He played a rock-concert-bound camper who gets mauled by a bear, with a total on-screen time of less than fifteen minutes.

Still, it was his first featured role. And for that it will always live in memory.

During the same year, Charlie auditioned for writer/director Oliver Stone's long-planned (ten years!) *Platoon*, but lost out to a slightly older, more experienced actor: his brother, Emilio. Of course, that circumstance later changed. And so did the early rivalry between the two. Emilio had been a better student in high school and the first of the family to have a successful acting career. It was even because Emilio took the family name, Estevez, said Charlie, that he decided to use Sheen—just to be different. (And also because he liked the way it sounded better.)

Eventually, after his own turn in *Platoon*, Charlie felt on a par with his brother; he was able to tell the press, "As soon as I became a professional peer, we got along great."

The *Platoon* casting process was unusual in that both brothers vied for the same role. Even though Martin, Emilio, and Charlie often look like clones to many fans, all but indistinguishable from one another, that's not usually the way the casting directors see it.

"My whole family is entirely supportive of one another and we're there to help each other out," noted Charlie. "Maybe if we were up for the same parts it would be different, but we're all different types." And that surprising statement was proven out when the two brothers auditioned for their next project.

Late in 1983, the siblings were slated to play brothers in John Milius's *Red Dawn*. But before production began, Milius recast Patrick Swayze as Charlie's older brother—he felt that the unrelated actor looked more like family! Charlie ended up with the fourth lead role as Matt Eckert, one of the young fighters killed by Russians in this conservative's fantasy film. The movie became a box-office hit for Metro-Goldwyn-Meyer and United Artists, even though it was panned by the critics during its release in the summer of 1984. It continued as a popular cable-television attraction for some time, often considered a dark flipside to Brat Pack bonding pictures like *The Outsiders*.

By the time *Red Dawn* was in release, Charlie had made his television feature debut in the CBS drama *Silence of the Heart*, costarring with his "Point Dume Mafia" cohort, Chad Lowe. Interestingly, neither pal knew that the other was going to audition for the TV project until they bumped into each other at the casting offices. Fate keeps placing a guiding hand on Charlie's career choices, it seems. This turned out to be the first time the boys had accidentally crossed paths during acting auditions, and it also turned out to be magic.

As Sheen commented to reporter Erik Knutzen, "We had the parts the minute we walked in together, before even reading . . . as soon as we mentioned we were best friends, we had it nailed on the spot. It was pure timing—it either kills you or it works for you."

Charlie played Ken Kruz, the best buddy of a teenager (Chad Lowe) who commits suicide because of mounting pressures from school and his peers. The production also starred Mariette Hartley and Howard Hesseman as the distraught parents.

Going back to films, Charlie had to pass up an offer from Emilio to make a cameo appearance in elder brother's behind-the-camera debut, *That Was Then . . . This Is Now*, because he was already signed to costar with Maxwell Caulfield in the unsettling New World Pictures release, *The Boys Next Door*. This not-very-well-remembered action-drama focused on two very angry, very alienated high school misfits—both with the boy-next-door look—who escalate from insensitive pranks to fatal violence during a weekend in Los Angeles following their graduation from a suburban high school.

One critic commented, "Maxwell Caulfield . . . is mesmerizing and sexually magnetic as an all-American psychopath. He's well-matched with the more subtly intense Charlie Sheen, son of Martin and young brother of Emilio Estevez."

Vincent Canby of *The New York Times* likewise could not praise Sheen's performance as Bo Richards without noting his lineage: "It's also exceptionally well-acted . . . by Mr. Sheen, still another talented acting son of Martin Sheen." Canby also noted that "the film is as chilling as Terrence Malick's *Badlands*, if not as poetic."

Perhaps it was the Sheen name that reminded him of that earlier film, which starred Martin and first introduced nine-year-old Charlie to producer Malick. The two had become fast friends, and Malick often offered the youngster encouragement, support, and even professional criticism of the boy's Super-8 shorts.

By March of 1985, Charlie was embarking on yet another feature film, *Lucas*, in which he plays a high school football hero (Cappie Roew) who protects the nerdish but endearing Lucas (Corey Haim) from the school bullies— and accidentally falls for Maggie (Kerri Green), the object of Lucas's devotion.

"With some actresses," Charlie later said, "there's a problem of no emotional chemistry. In this case, my infatuation was essentially real." (Those sparks would come in handy once again, when Charlie would have a slightly more mature romance with actress Green in the 1986 feature *Three for the Road*.)

Sheen learned that he was cast for 20th Century Fox's *Lucas* just two weeks before filming began. He was vacationing in Hawaii at the time, and immediately went to work. He started on an intensive training program with former San Francisco 49er Merv Lopez, and he was having a ball. Finally, a chance for his love of sports to coexist with an acting career! It could even be an advantage, he discovered to his glee. He began pumping iron to bulk up a bit.

Combining sports and acting brought out the best in Sheen. The writer-director of *Lucas* positively fell in love with him. "Charlie has a wonderful sense of humor," extoled David Seltzer. "A detached sense of irony. He can laugh at himself. He can laugh at the world without really doing it overtly.

"You sense that Charlie really doesn't take himself all that seriously, and that's a pleasure to watch on-screen because leading men are terribly serious, self-righteous, and pompous. Charlie is the antithesis of all this. He really is a joker. It's that quality we all love in Burt Reynolds."

Lucas producer David Niksay agreed: "He has a great, offhand sense of humor that is very captivating. He's also very confident in the way he ultimately plays a scene, and that confidence comes, I believe, from having been able to watch good actors all his life, internalize their roles and make them real from within. He does this very naturally."

Of the film, Charlie commented, "It's about first love, growing up. It was an overindulgence in cuteness, but a good experience."

You could come up with a pretty similar two-line description of *Ferris Bueller's Day Off*, a wildly popular summer youth picture from the John Hughes factory, in which Charlie performed a one-scene cameo that set the screen to sizzling. It was that one scene that probably generated more attention to his "smolder" than all the work that went before—and he only did it because he's a friend and fan of the film's star, Matthew Broderick.

That small part won a lot of attention, and from some unusual corners. After his enormous success in 1987, Charlie told *In Fashion* magazine that "the first time I really felt like people knew who I was was when I picked up *MAD* magazine and they were doing a parody of *Ferris Bueller* and there I was in the artwork. I thought, this is kind of cool. *MAD* magazine, a magazine I grew up worshipping, and they've got my ugly ass in there gracing the pages. Forget the Oscars, forget great films and performances, forget all the hoopla—that really stood out for me."

During the fall of 1985, Charlie was able to play alongside his father in a walk-on role in the television movie *Out of Darkness*. Martin portrayed a detective pursuing a psychotic killer. "I was supposed to be some guy living in a building my father's character is checking out," said Charlie. "He knocks on the door, I open it—with shaving cream all over my face and my hair greased back—then slam it shut.

"It's terrific to play with my dad."

Charlie's cameo in *Wisdom*, written and directed by Emilio, was quite another matter—as was his starring role in the now-you-see-it, now-you-don't science-fiction thriller, *The Wraith*. Charlie commented to *People* magazine early in 1987 that "it's [*The Wraith*] probably double-billing with *Wisdom* right now on malfunctioning airplanes." Later, he went so far as to say, "I have the distinction of having starred in possibly one of the worst movies of all time."

In *The Wraith*, Sheen starred as Jake Kesey, a new boy in town who has a very mysterious past. Turns out that he's his own avenging angel, coming back to his hometown to even a score and pick up his old girlfriend. Jake's destined for a head-on confrontation with Nick Cassavetes, who plays Packard Walsh, the ruthless leader of a sadistic, drug-addicted gang of road pirates who steal cars through terrorist tactics and murder for the fun of it.

Wraith producer John Kemeny—who also has the more respectable efforts *Quest for Fire* and *Atlantic City* to his credit—said of his leading men: "Charlie and Nick have as charismatic a screen presence as any young actors I've ever worked with. They are going to be big stars. I knew that when I worked with Richard Dreyfuss on his first starring role in *The Apprenticeship of Duddy Kravitz*, and I know that now with these boys. When either of them has the scene the screen just comes alive."

Perhaps the most notable aspect of *The Wraith* was its cast of show-business offspring. Nick Cassavetes is the son of Gena Rowlands and John Cassavetes; gang member Griffin O'Neal is Ryan O'Neal's son; Clint Howard, also in the gang, is actor-director Ron Howard's younger brother; and Randy (Sheriff Loomis) Quaid was celebrated as an actor before his brother, Dennis, made it big in 1987.

Sheen admitted that his character came fairly easily to him, because it was probably closer to his own personality than the roles some of his costars had to tackle. Or, perhaps, one could say that his estimation of the character revealed some of his self-image at the time.

Charlie told the unit publicist: "Jake is the type of guy who is a lot like myself. He's pretty mellow, good-natured. When there's as much of me as there is in Jake, I just look within myself. I love playing character roles and I like to play a wide range of characters. But I also enjoy just fitting real comfortably into a role like this. I guess [producers] Mike Marvin and John Kemeny must have sensed some similarities between Jake and myself when they hired me. So that's how I played him."

The end of 1985 was a time for self-examination on Charlie's part. He was taking a look at his career decisions, and taking a look back at the decisions he had made earlier in life. He told an interviewer from *Seventeen* magazine: "I've got a better perspective now. If I had known the importance of learning how to deal with people, I would have borne a little more. But I felt I was never going to get out. I thought I'd be in high school for the rest of my life. I never had any patience.

"Now I see the educational structure is very similar to a lot of what I'm involved with professionally. Someone's always going to have the upper hand; being an actor, you're essentially your own boss, but if you're not producing your own films, you still have to be hired."

Having paid his proverbial dues as a newly working actor, Charlie Sheen was ready for the biggest role of his career thus far. Just two weeks after *The Wraith* wrapped, he was on his way to the Philippines where, as fate continued to nudge, he was to play the narrator-lead in a Vietnam War epic . . . just as his father had done a decade before.

But, as the elder Sheen said, "He was a grunt, and I was an officer. How can you compare us?"

▪ 17 ▪

Back to the Jungle

PLATOON WAS THE EIGHTH FILM OF CHARLIE SHEEN'S CAREER and his fifth starring role in a four-year period. It was the movie that would make him a major star. Yet, in spite of his lifelong experience in the business, once he arrived at the shooting location he was nearly as naive as Private First Class Chris Taylor, the idealistic young soldier he portrayed.

When Charlie stepped from the plane, he immediately recognized the "mildew scent" of the jungle he had known ten years earlier, back when he joined his father during the filming of *Apocalypse Now*. "I got hit in the face with that odor—this weird and powerful smell like burning rubber and malaria and poverty and rot. . . . The whole thing was a strange homecoming, just like walking back into a bad dream all over again," he told reporter Elvis Mitchell.

In that original bad dream, Charlie was more the observer of tragedy—Martin's stress- and chain-smoking-induced heart attack and nervous breakdown—than he was a firsthand victim. This time around, Charlie would be the

131

star of his own nightmare. Along with the jungle stench, Charlie would learn the true meaning of blood, sweat, and tears, that would be indelibly stamped in his memory.

Oscar-winning *Platoon* was based on Oliver Stone's firsthand experiences as a grunt (foot soldier) with the 25th Infantry during the early peak of the Vietnam conflict, 1967–68. The writer-director explained, "I wanted to explore the everyday realities of what it was like to be a nineteen-year-old boy in the bush for the first time. The story is based on experiences I had over there in three different combat units, and the characters are people I knew during the war."

Stone wrote the screenplay for *Platoon* ten years before it went into production. "It was rejected everywhere," he said. "I think it was too harsh a look at the war—too grim and realistic."

During that frustrating decade of rejection, Stone did manage to win an Academy Award and a Writers Guild Award for the screenplay of *Midnight Express*. He also wrote or co-wrote such other major films as *Conan the Barbarian* and *Scarface*, and directed the much-praised *Salvador* (starring James Woods) from his own script. After ten years, *Platoon* "suddenly" became recognized as a viable project by a proven and highly touted professional.

Although both Charlie and his brother Emilio have insisted that any early competitiveness between them was short-lived, this project was one on which they definitely competed. It turned out to be an issue that eventually resolved itself without rancor. When Oliver Stone was first auditioning actors for *Platoon* in late 1983, he chose Emilio from the two brothers because he was more physically filled out and a bit more mature than Charlie at the time.

Charlie, a fan of Stone's writing on *Midnight Express* and *Scarface*, was openly disappointed. He loved the *Platoon* script the moment he read it, and wanted to be a part of the production. The fates were on his side once again. Financing for the project fell through and production was put on hold for nearly two more years. During that time, Charlie grew from gangly teen to young adult, and polished his talents through several other productions. By the time the *Platoon* cameras were set to role, Charlie was ready . . . and Emilio was unavailable.

Charlie knew that the preparations for his part would require a back-to-basic-training approach, but he didn't realize how basic. "I thought they would put us in a barracks, and everyone would have a radio, telephones," he recalled. "We'd do a few hours of physical training a day, take showers, have hot catered meals, then study our scripts. I couldn't have been more wrong!"

After one night in a hotel, Charlie remembered arriving by bus at an open clearing in the jungle some sixty miles outside of Manila in the Philippines. There the actors, wearing baggy fatigues and jungle boots, were issued dog tags, rifles, bayonets, ponchos, poncho liners, flashlights (with red filters for night use), four canteens per man, assorted hand weapons, and a heavy load of other infantry gear. Charlie, like each of the others, toted seventy pounds of equipment wherever he went. And they were given shovels.

The first order to the estimable cast of this Hollywood extravaganza: Start digging! Their foxholes became home for the next two weeks of intensive training. Charlie admitted almost a year later that his first response was, "Dig what? Can I get my agent on the phone?" All the men (actors from California, Tennessee, New York, Texas, and the Philippines) were put through the rigors of a normally eleven-week basic-training course in a fraction of that time. "We didn't eat properly or shower for two weeks," Charlie recalled.

The Hemdale Film Corporation and Orion Pictures hired a retired Marine captain, Dale Dye, to turn some thirty actors (with a wide variety of backgrounds and origins) into the soldiers they would become on-screen, like it or not.

As if that weren't bad enough, some of Sheen's castmates, and even Oliver Stone, were already anticipating Sheen to be a spoiled, rich surfer from Malibu. According to Charlie, someone had contacted Stone to warn him about the young star's personal habits.

"Oliver was urged not to hire me," Charlie told *Los Angeles Times* reporter Roderick Mann. "It was suggested that I drank while I worked, which just isn't true. . . . Oliver made me agree to have only one beer a day while we were in the Philippines. But by the end of the fourth week, he was so pleased with my work he was buying me drinks at the bar."

Drinking wasn't the only bad habit of Charlie's that *Platoon* reinforced. Ironically, it was Stone who started Charlie smoking cigarettes, because he felt it was an appropriate part of Sheen's film character. It's a habit he hasn't been able to break since.

Oliver Stone wasn't the only person who worried that Charlie wouldn't be rough-hewn enough for his part. Fellow actor Willem Dafoe expressed his own trepidation to *US* magazine: "We expected this little creep . . . He got pampered a little. He was younger. . . . His mother packed him eight hundred boxes of things. You imagined he'd really cry foul when things got down and dirty, but he really got his nose in there."

Charlie's metamorphosis from beach brat to rugged Rambo came through a series of personal challenges, even insults. Charlie told *People* magazine about a scene in which he was unloading a helicopter and wanted to wear a tee shirt to protect his torso from rocks and dirt kicked up by the chopper. Stone wanted the shirt off; Sheen wanted it on. Stone turned on him and said, "What? Are you a pussy?

Are you a little pussy from Malibu? Played too much volleyball all your life?''

At that point, Charlie's hair-trigger temper was ignited. ''I got so pissed off I ripped the shirt off, did the scene . . . and had scars on my back for weeks.''

Sheen admitted that by the second day of training, he and several other actors had already been pushed to the edge of mutiny. ''We got together and said, 'We're actors, not infantry. Let's just walk.' ''

But there's a certain joy and pride that comes from being pushed to one's limits. Of the training, Charlie has since boasted, ''We were asked to do things way beyond the realm of our experience. I think we got as close as we could to the real thing, without being in a life-and-death situation.''

Dale Dye knew what he was doing. ''I set up a training program that was intentionally difficult and physically demanding,'' he explained during filming. ''I believe that the only way a man can portray the rigors of jungle combat is to get a taste of it.''

Dye's training program also included the taste of Army rations twice each day. The plastic-wrapped meals, called Ready-to-Eat, were precooked hamburgers, small cold hot dogs, and ''bean something,'' as Charlie dubbed it.

Each day the actors were kept busy from 5:30 in the morning until late at night with classes on M-16 automatic rifle set-up and breakdown, squad-radio procedures, calisthenics, and the much-dreaded full-gear patrols—including several eighteen-kilometer uphill-downhill backbreakers. All of this in 100-degree heat, drenching humidity, sticky dusty dirt, swarms of red ants, and ''students'' at the point of complete exhaustion. War is hell, and the cast soon learned that making this movie would be hell, too.

''The idea of the cram course was to immerse the actors into the infantryman's life—his way of thinking, talking, and moving,'' explained Stone, who was wounded twice and received the Bronze Star during his combat service in Vietnam. "I hoped that subconsciously what would slip out would be the dog-tired, don't-give-a-damn attitude, the anger, frustration, casual brutality, and the way death was approached. These are the assets and liabilities of infantrymen.

"I remember being so tired that I wished the N.V.A. (North Vietnamese Army) would come up and shoot me and get this thing over with."

For Captain Dye, the line between make-believe and cold, hard reality became blurred for a few brief, frightening days.

"Late in the training session, the platoon went out on an overnight hump [hike]," he recalled. "They became disoriented . . . lost in a deep part of the jungle, which is easy to understand if you know the type of terrain. The only way out of their position was to scale a sheer rock wall."

Back at the base camp, Dye received word by radio from one of his ex-Marine assistants that the platoon was about to make that attempt.

"I was scared," Dye admitted. "I thought, 'I hope to hell we haven't gone too far.' But I knew that if they just relied on the training we'd been through, they could gut it out."

They did. And when the actors-turned-infantrymen wearily arrived back at base camp, Dye (who became an infantryman-turned-actor as Captain Harris in the film) advised them to remember and to use that sense of real danger in their performances.

On graduation day, the actors' platoon was up at dawn for its first day of filming in a rain forest. There was no break for anyone, no first shower in two weeks, no rest or the comfort of a good night's sleep on a soft bed. The last day of training completely blurred into the first day of actual filming.

The Philippines Constabulary, an organization much like the United States' Green Berets, was called into film action. They became the "bad guys" in the staged attack on the platoon that would test all that the actors had learned during their training. The test attack proved all too real . . . all but fatal, as it turned out.

Charlie remembered that someone "had his compass readings all screwed up, and he led us about five hours off course. When we finally got back on track, we were so tired that when the attack came they shot the shit out of us. I was deafened by a charge that went off. I fell to the ground; a smoke grenade landed in my crotch. I looked down at my groin and there was this device spewing fire and smoke. Luckily, I wasn't hurt.

"The program they put us through represented two of the longest, craziest, toughest weeks of my life."

On many occasions since, Sheen has commented, "My respect for the real Vietnam vets has escalated seven hundred percent. I wouldn't have survived two days in that war."

And his respect for Stone ranks almost as high for him as a director as for his war record. Sheen told interviewer Leonora Langley: "Oliver knew just the right buttons to push. He'd piss you off at times and he'd be very compassionate at others. He really knows how to get into you and pull things out. He's so in touch with his own reality. Outside of my father, he's the most brutally honest person I've ever met in my life. Whether he's acting or directing, he tells it as it is."

Platoon ended up grossing more than $130 million in the United States alone in one year. It won Academy Awards for Best Picture, Best Director, Best Film Editing, and Best Sound, and had also been nominated in the categories of Best Supporting Actor (for both Tom Berenger and Willem Dafoe), Best Cinematography, and Best Original Screenplay. "While we knew we were capturing certain moments during the making of the movie, we had no idea what impact it would have. We didn't know Oliver was going to put it together that brilliantly and that the public would accept it so insanely,'' said Charlie.

"In my estimation," he added, beginning to sound truly like his father's son, "*Platoon* also helped to bring home the fact that we could see ourselves in future situations such as El Salvador, Nicaragua, and Grenada, where similar political climates might explode. Hopefully, kids my age will never have to die for a cause of which they aren't even aware.

"I certainly stand by my country in most things, but there's no way in hell that I'd sign up should there be another Vietnam. If they think they can remove my rights as a human and thrust me into a situation of that caliber, they're going to get a fight—that's if they can locate me!"

• 18 •

Back Home Again

POST-COMBAT STRESS FATIGUE PLAGUED CHARLIE FOR SEVERAL
months after returning from *Platoon*'s Philippine location.
In a conversation with journalist Leonora Langley, Sheen
admitted, "It was tough coming back into the real world.
There are no law courts, traffic lights, or sophisticated
utensils out there."

Bottom line: The Charlie Sheen who came back from
the "war" was not the same kid who left for it. Not only
had *Platoon* marked his graduation into box-office success
and industry recognition, but it endowed him with a new
sense of balance and maturity. One of the first changes the
young man made on his return was to move out of his
family's Malibu home and find a place of his own for the
first time. He bought a two-story beachfront townhouse.

But the emotional adjustment was not as simple as a
physical move. Charlie explained, "When I came home, I
was thinking, 'Hey, where are my guys, where's my
platoon?' I was depressed for about a month after I got

back. I was just walking around, lost in space because everything had been so exciting.''

Charlie tried a number of things to blow off some of the steam. One of them was yet another armed-combat-with-props: commercial war games where businessmen dress up as soldiers and shoot red-paint ''blood'' at each other. But that wasn't enough to salve the frayed edges of Charlie's emotions. ''I had a hard time being hunted down by lawyers and agents after fighting the N.V.A. for nine weeks. It was a bit dubious, you know. What are they gonna do, throw a deposition at me?

''It was just tough to come down from everything. I mean, you can't just veg out and watch *Wheel of Fortune*.''

It goes to show how viscerally all that action hit young Sheen; after all, weren't those very N.V.A. soldiers only another group of soft-bottomed actors? What would they have thrown at him, scripts? But to him, it was all too real.

A young lady, actress Dolly Fox, was a part of Charlie's life and *Platoon* experience during this period. After five weeks in the jungle, he called her in Los Angeles and asked her to join him in the Philippines. That's where ''she became my girlfriend,'' he said. ''That turned out to be really helpful, because she was there with me for that crucial readjustment time when I came back.'' However, that romance ran its course and ended with unkind words.

Eventually, with enough help from (and partying with) old friends like Chris Penn, Tom Howell, and others; heavy doses of music from his rock'n'roll heroes (Led Zeppelin, Jimi Hendrix, The Doors, The Police, and U-2); some stress-release bodybuilding; writing poetry and practicing yoga; Sheen settled back into his California lifestyle. And then he was off to Little Rock, Arkansas for his next feature-film project.

Three for the Road, a film Sheen called ''a fun little story,'' was his first adult romantic comedy. He portrays

Paul Tracey, an ambitious political aide whose idealistic dedication leads him to misplace his trust in the self-centered Senator Ketteredge (actor Raymond J. Barry).

Kerri Green, who previously starred with Sheen in *Lucas*, plays Senator Ketteredge's neglected daughter, Robin. Spending time with an acting buddy who hadn't been crawling through the Philippine jungle with him was a relief for Charlie. He and Green were often spotted tossing a baseball to each other between scenes—a far cry from shooting down North Vietnamese.

During this period, Charlie's own 16mm film, *RPG*, was used in Emilio's movie *Wisdom*, and he wrote, directed, and produced a music video called *Nicks* as well. On top of that, the multitalented young star completed a script for a comedy called *How to Eat and Drive*, a fantasy about the American Dream that he wants to direct.

"Getting into all aspects of the business is the only way to go," said Charlie, taking a bit of advice from his brother Emilio, whom he respects immensely. "I too often find myself on the set knowing there's a lot better way of going about something. I want to be the captain of the ship and run the whole show."

Charlie's next project was a film called *No Man's Land*. His character, Ted Varrick, is the head of a multimillion-dollar Porsches-only auto-theft ring. He also runs a nightspot called Club Babylon, which, said Charlie, "is sort of a 'Lifestyles of the Rich and Aimless' hangout." He was particularly thrilled to have played the bad guy this time.

"At first they wanted me to play the cop," recalled Sheen. "That was somehow the obvious choice; they felt the audience would be expecting to see me in that role. I had to audition three times on videotape," to convince the producers to give him a shot at being the bad guy.

"I don't want to do the same kind of character every time out," he explained. "Finally, after a lot of hemming and hawing about it, they said all right."

The role of the undercover cop, Benjy Taylor, went to young up-and-comer D.B. Sweeney, who had his doubts about working with the already notorious young Sheen. "I was worried," Sweeney admitted. "I thought that he might be another Malibu baby, but he turned out to be a regular guy."

Of course, had Charlie played the cop, it's less likely that he'd have that six-stitch scar on his lower jaw today. "The ironic thing," said Charlie, "is that I went through *Platoon* without getting more than a scratch!"

The accident happened while Sheen was filming a chase scene in an underground parking garage. He was running from two of the film's characters who were firing their guns at him. Special effects were being used to show bullets missing Sheen and hitting a nearby car. Explosives were hidden inside the cars and predrilled "bullet holes" were covered up with bonding material. The special-effects team ignited the explosives, the bonding blew off with a nice "poof," and, *voila!* bullet hole. It was debris from the bonding material that cut Charlie's chin.

According to one detailed tabloid report: "Martin was on the set and was among the first to get to Charlie, who was conscious but bleeding from his jaw. . . . Martin was so upset that he refused to wait until an ambulance was called, and drove like a bat out of hell from the location site to Cedars Sinai Medical Center. When they got to the hospital, he turned to Charlie, whose face was as white as a sheet. Charlie reached over, pulled the keys out of the ignition, and said: 'Dad, you drive like an idiot. I thought you were going to get us killed any moment!' "

No Man's Land did more for Charlie than make him aware of the hazards of special effects. It also made him more aware of the hazards of owning a Porsche—and he is the proud owner of a 1987 sports model. He learned a lot about his vehicle while making the film—specifically, how easy it is to steal one (or any other high-end foreign car, for that matter) in about thirty seconds flat.

"As part of the research for the role we were assigned to watch a professional car thief," Sheen said. "It took him twelve seconds to get into the car, ten seconds to kill the alarm and find the ignition switch, ten more seconds to fire it up and drive away. Total: thirty-two seconds. He's retired now," Charlie said of the pro.

Give somebody like Charlie a big paycheck and a souped-up car, and you know there's going to be some kind of behind-the-scenes adventure. In this case, it was a high-speed test drive.

"One night," recalled Charlie, "after breaking the car in, I said, 'I'm going to see what's under the hood of this sucker.' It was three o'clock in the morning, no traffic lights, I hadn't had a drink all day. I was totally wide-awake. There's a straightaway on Pacific Coast Highway that runs for about four miles past Trancas to the county line. I got it up to a hundred and thirty miles an hour—up to where the white line is no longer separated—and that was pretty scary. I knew I had some left in the car, but I didn't know how much I had left in me. I slowed down, and I haven't done it since. But just being on the edge for that moment was exciting."

Directly after wrapping *No Man's Land*, Charlie began work on another Oliver Stone film, *Wall Street*, which fate had decided would be released only weeks after the Big Crash of October 1987. Charlie played Bud Fox, a young stock trader, and Martin played his on-screen father, "a decent man forced to bear witness to his son's rise and fall." The cast for the big Christmas movie included Michael Douglas (who received an Oscar nomination for Best Actor) and Daryl Hannah.

Charlie and Martin had acted together before, in television. But *Wall Street* was the first time the two shared the big screen. Charlie admitted having mixed feelings about working with his father, who came in to do his two weeks of work after the rest of the cast had already worked nine weeks on the film and was exhausted.

"He kind of pulled us together and made us look like a bunch of amateurs," Charlie said ruefully. "Working with my father, I found I'd get discouraged by the thought that maybe I'm not going to be this good some day. Then I'd be encouraged to think maybe I will be. . . . He's definitely the best guy I know, as a father and as an individual."

Working together was an emotional experience for both men. It brought back old memories and further tightened already strong bonds. "We weren't nervous at all. Dad is never nervous," Charlie boasted to journalist Tom Green. "There's a scene in the hospital where he's had a heart attack. I go in there and we're both breaking down. I remember what it was like after my dad really did have a heart attack, nearly a decade ago. I mean, we connected, man. We connected in five minutes where some fathers and sons don't connect in a lifetime."

Working with Oliver Stone again, Charlie began to respect that man more and more as a father figure as well. It was a time of connections in all directions. "I sense that he sees things in me that he vicariously enjoys because his youth wasn't lived as fully as mine is being now," Charlie has said of Stone. "There are a couple of things I'd like to do that I haven't done and I might not. Still, I can do most of the things I want. I'm happy about, oh, seventy percent of the time, which isn't bad.

"In directing me," Charlie continued, "we really connected. It's not like he had to pull me aside and reiterate the script to me. Very few words are spoken; sometimes it's just a look. I think we're going to do a few more [films] together."

The Charlie the audience saw in *Wall Street* was hardly the callow youth of *Lucas* or even the old-beyond-his-years infantryman of *Platoon*. It was also hardly the Charlie his friends and family know. This was a high-energy businessman who's supposed to be a bit older than Sheen's actual age. A sophisticated wardrobe was only part of the makeover needed to mold Charlie to the part. He gained a few pounds; he developed a character much different than himself. "I've always had a kind of laid-back existence in my general demeanor," said Charlie. "There's a kind of a relaxed quality about my life. I don't like to get uptight about things, and try to avoid ulcers and heart attacks and hemorrhoids and all that.

"For this part I had to increase the pace of my speech and maintain an intense level of clarity and deal with all the financial stuff. I never even got through math! But Oliver kept saying, 'It's working.' He had to be the consummate director on this film, and I had to surrender to him."

During one of many dozen interviews about his role as an amoral stock jock, Sheen admitted, "So far, Bud Fox has been the toughest role of my career. It has a lot of quick dialogue, a lot of intense, edgy emotions. To me, that's much more difficult to put across than the extreme emotions of a soldier on the battlefield. It may be oversimplifying, but what was my role in *Platoon*, really? It was one every boy acts out as a kid, playing war. It's harder to give a convincing portrayal of an average guy."

Following *Wall Street* but before jumping into his next feature film, Charlie made his directorial debut with an independent short film, *RPG II*, a sequel to his first 16mm *RPG*. In the first story, a low-budget moviemaker blows up a Fotomat with a rocket-propelled grenade because he can't get his film back from the neighborhood stand. In the sequel—a 35mm project made in the summer of 1986 and starring bodybuilder/scholar Dolph (*He-Man*) Lundgren—he blows up a lifeguard stand. There has been talk of featuring the two short films on cassette for the home-video market.

Then, in mid-1987, Charlie got a chance to combine his two greatest loves when he was reunited with his *No Man's Land* costar, D.B. Sweeney, in *Eight Men Out*. The movie is about the "Black Sox" scandal of 1919—when the Chicago White Sox were influenced by gamblers to throw the World Series—and casts both young men as baseball players.

Sweeney welcomed the opportunity to work with Charlie again. In addition to their current acting careers, the two young men share similar high school memories. Like Charlie, Sweeney had been an aspiring baseball jock in high school. However, a motorcycle accident tore up Sweeney's knee and dashed his professional sports ambitions.

Perhaps playing a baseball player rather than playing baseball was the right thing for Charlie in the long run. At least, he thinks so. Recalling his lost baseball scholarship and missed opportunity to be the ace of the diamond, he said, "Even if the baseball opportunity had come through, I wouldn't have lasted more than a couple of years on the college team. Too many guys out there need to make it. I didn't; it wasn't my way out. Acting always felt comfortable."

Interestingly, this was a second project in which Charlie was the second choice for the part: Originally, Emilio was to have played Buck Weaver in the film. Just as had happened in *Platoon*, Emilio had been picked for the role during the film's long genesis. For two years he was attached to the production, and by time the project was finally in preparation, he had to drop out in favor of other commitments. Again, the role went to his kid brother.

Passing up his father's suggestion to do Shakespeare's *Henry IV, Part I* in New York with producer Joseph Papp ("I'm just not ready for the stage"), Charlie next went into production as the star of *Johnny Utah*, an F.B.I. adventure tale for Columbia Pictures scheduled for a late 1988 release.

Has life in the fast lane—and in the spotlight—taken its toll on this Sheen? He says not. "I'm still a regular guy," he declared to *Cosmopolitan* magazine. "I go to the batting cage at Dodger games. I hang out with my girlfriends. And I go to the beach. It's not as fast-paced as it must look on the exterior.

"If you're going to party and knock yourself out, and that works for you, fine," he said on another occasion. "It doesn't work for me. What's nice about being committed on a film is you don't drink, you don't stay out till all hours. If you choose to do those things when you finish, then it's just that much more enjoyable.

"I've been very fortunate in avoiding the Hollywood elements—drugs, seductions, the general craziness. I'm pretty good—actually, I'm very good—about drawing the line. I'm in a position when I'm working that ninety-eight percent of SAG [Screen Actors Guild] would like to be in. I think I've maintained the perspective of not jeopardizing that position. That would be unfair to me, and unfair to those who could be there if they had a clear mind."

▪ 19 ▪

Charlie's Angels

TIMES CHANGE. WHEN TWENTY-YEAR-OLD MARTIN SHEEN began dating Janet Templeton, he was still a virgin. Considering Sheen's very Roman Catholic sense of morality, it was quite daring and rather bohemian that they should have decided to live together for a year before they got married.

Today's Estevez-Sheen dynasty keeps up with (and possibly, ahead of) the times. At nineteen, Charlie fathered his first child. At the end of the same year, 1984, older brother Emilio—then twenty-two—fathered his first son. Two years later, Emilio had a daughter by the mother of his son. But neither modern male has traded in his little black book for a band of gold.

While both boys have since severed romantic relationships with their children's mothers, grandparents Martin and Janet have done their best to maintain family cohesiveness. According to one family friend, "Janet and Marty have set both mothers up with homes of their own and

149

have helped their sons handle both the financial and emotional responsibilities. Of course, both boys are now financially secure, but it's been Marty and Janet who really preserve the idea of family between them all.''

When his daughter Cassandra was not quite three years old, Charlie told a reporter, ''It's nothing I'm ashamed of. I see her every weekend. I can't let her get to be ten years old and say, 'Who's Daddy?' I couldn't live with that. That's the stuff you go to hell for.'' Living on the Hollywood fast track, Charlie has seen enough broken homes to know how devastating their effect can be. He wants, in his own way, the best for his little girl.

With fame and fortune and obvious good looks, Charlie certainly has no lack of willing women surrounding him, be he a father or not. His blatant sex appeal prompted one publication, *US* magazine, to claim he has ''an Indy 500 sex drive off-screen.'' *People* magazine made a point of noting that his not-so-little black book includes more than two dozen ladies' names and numbers. Each entry is marked with Sheen's highly descriptive rating system. Sometimes, Charlie seems a bit callow—even callous—about the women in his life. Once he described his parting with a former flame thusly: ''I had a girlfriend, but I got that piano off my back.''

Perhaps Charlie just likes the rather gruff and macho playboy image. But much of it is just that: an image, an act. Because if he were that heartless, would former love Dolly Fox remain so loyal to the privacy of their relationship and kind in her response about Charlie's family? Said Fox, ''I lived with Charlie for nine months and lived with the Sheen family, too, for a while. The whole family is wonderful. They are all the most special people I have ever met. I respect them, and I love them all very much. They became like my family. Ramon—he's so special and a really wonderful, wonderful person—and Renee are still two of my closest friends.''

Without displaying any animosity whatsoever, Fox said, "Of course, I hesitate to talk about Charlie. We had a really rough breakup. It was ugly . . . after being together for so long. *Platoon* was not the only location I was on with Charlie; there were four all together. But the relationship is private and not something I feel I should talk about."

Since the summer of 1987, Charlie has been enjoying a romantic liaison with British actress-model Charlotte Lewis. The exotic Chilean-Iranian ingenue has been working as a model since she was twelve years old, but the American public knows her best for her roles in *Pirates* with Walter Matthau and *The Golden Child* with Eddie Murphy. Society column (and tabloid) readers will already know that she's dated Murphy, Mikhail Baryshnikov, and director Roman Polanski before getting involved with Charlie Sheen at the tender age of twenty.

Lewis had first noticed the handsome actor on-screen in *Platoon*. She admitted, "I actually saw *Platoon* three times before I met him. And I remember thinking, 'This guy is gorgeous! How come I never met him when I was in Los Angeles making *Golden Child*?' I never get to meet any of the young, attractive actors of today. I'm always hidden behind some palm, studying. It's not fair!"

Whether it was written in the stars (Lewis consults clairvoyants and astrologers on a regular basis) or simply coincidence, Charlie and Charlotte met one week after she arrived in Los Angeles in search of more American roles. Instead, she landed one of the most sought-after American males.

"I was invited to a dinner party," Lewis recalled. "Charlie was there. It was just, 'Hello, how are you?' and I went 'Bong!' We were really attracted to each other. It's only been three months, but it's been a kind of intense three months," she qualified at the time.

In a page right out of a romance novel, it turned out that

Charlie had been attracted to Charlotte before ever meeting her, as well. "I'd seen a picture of Charlotte in the back of *Playboy* magazine—not nude or anything. I cut it out and put it in my wallet because I thought she as an amazing-looking girl." He was coaxed to the fateful dinner party, as it turned out, by a friend who teased, "You might meet the girl of your dreams!"

Charlie admitted later, "It clicked immediately. I didn't want to come on like some schmuck, so I laid back and said, 'Good night' to her." The next day, Charlotte and Charlie went to the beach and a baseball game and from the start Charlie said to himself, "I'm taken. This boy is gone!" However (surprise, surprise), he still makes no noises about marriage plans. "I have the rest of my life for marriage," he said recently.

"We're not just girlfriend-boyfriend," Charlotte has insisted. "We're good friends. We have an honest relationship, which is the way I have relationships—the way it has to be if it's going to be something that's going to last."

Charlotte has always been linked to older men, so Sheen is a different, youthful energy in her life. Even her female friends have always been older. "My best girlfriend is about forty," she said. "I often wondered what I would do with younger people . . . that was the only thing with Charlie that I worried about: He's young; what will we have in common? Of course, we have everything in common because we are both young! I had just never given it a chance before.

"Charlie's the youngest man I've ever known, which is very strange for me because he's almost the most mature man I've ever known. He's very young but he's very intelligent and he's very wise."

Charlie's latest angel gets along well with the Estevez-Sheen clan. "They're all very nice, very friendly to me." Of Charlie's daughter and Emilio's two children, Charlotte—

whose own unwed mother became pregnant with her at age twenty-eight—found the family's arrangements "kind of commendable when you think about it."

One of the first things Charlotte did after meeting Charlie was to have his astrological chart made up, discovering that "he's a very strong person," which is just fine with her.

"I could never be with a man unless he was strong," she said. "I'd be bored with him in a minute. I'm still old-fashioned; the man is the dominant party. That's just how I like it. Charlie's a very strong person and there's no competition. We're very compatible. There's no 'I'm stronger than you are,' because he admires me and I admire him. I need somebody who's got drive, who's intelligent, somebody who has ambition. You've got to be able to learn from each other."

Charlotte loves to talk about Charlie, and is abundantly effusive about his accomplishments. But she has still found it somewhat odd that they get along together as well as they do. "It's funny," she said. "Charlie doesn't know anything about my life. He doesn't know London. He hasn't met my mother. He doesn't know any of my friends. My friends are all much older than me and scattered all over the world. So it must be kind of strange for him. I know everything about him—his friends since he was two years old, his family, where he was born and brought up.

"But we're very similar in many ways. I like the way he thinks. We know what each other thinks, because we have the same moods. I like that," Charlotte concluded.

Charlie, on his part, is delighted with his girlfriend because "she's really cool. I finally found a girl who doesn't want to overtake my life and usurp my existence . . . she really cuts me some slack." But he also admits that he isn't making future plans for them. "I'm one of those day-at-a-time guys," he has told interviewers.

Charlie does live what appears to be a freewheeling,

devil-may-care lifestyle with fast cars and beautiful women. But appearances aren't everything. This is also a young man who can be quiet and thoughtful and listen to his inner voices. Unlike Emilio, who measures his words oh-so-very-carefully for the press, Charlie occasionally allows his thoughts—even on touchy topics like man, woman, and God—to flow freely:

"Tomorrow, I could be Joe Axelby sitting naked on the beach and still be happy as long as I've got what's going on inside and I can trust myself," he said in a 1987 interview. "If you can't ring your own dinner bell, then you can't like or love anybody else. I have a strong desire to travel and maybe someday, when I'm about forty, I'll settle down and marry. I'd rather wait till the whole AIDS thing has run its course. It's all a bit brutal and scary.

"At the end of the day, I believe in the Force *à la* George Lucas, by which I mean there is a guiding, controlling, universal power that watches over us. I don't believe in a guy with a gray beard in a giant white chair telling us what our next move is going to be. If I get up there and I was wrong I apologize and, if not, what am I going to do?

"You could say I'm heavily into the lottery."

▪ 20 ▪

Ramon Sheen

OF THE THREE SHEEN BOYS, RAMON HAS BEEN KEEPING THE
lowest profile—so far. Middle sons have a way of doing
that. But when he arrived on this planet, Ramon did so
with a dramatic turn. It was while Martin and Janet were
living on Staten Island in New York; Emilio was a toddler,
and money was scarce. Martin decided to deliver this child
himself, in his living room.

"We were foolish," Martin reminisced in 1982. "We
were just a couple of kids. It was a big risk; we shouldn't
have done it; we were lucky. He was very large, and Janet
hemorrhaged, no doctor, nothing. I panicked, I took them
to the hospital in fright. On my way back, I'll never forget
the headlines—Mrs. [John F.] Kennedy had lost her baby
the same day."

Named for his father and now happily integrating both
the given and the stage names he inherited, Ramon also
grew up on film locations around the world. Although he
often ducked away from the lens of the kids' famous

155

Super-8 camera, he still was a witness to the moviemaking magic. But what he witnessed didn't always appeal to him.

"When I was growing up there was so much acting and filming going on around me," said Ramon, "that I decided that it wasn't for me. So I carved a niche for myself as the dancer-musician in the family. I always had roles in the family productions, but they were choreographed rather than directed."

Ramon continued to maintain his own individual style throughout high school. Of the three male offspring, Ramon's Santa Monica High School career was the most even-keeled. Schoolmate Cara Poston remembered: "Ramon was a lot more quiet and shy than either of his brothers. The three were each very different. Emilio was liked by everyone and was the most extroverted; Charlie never stopped talking about baseball and was particularly popular with the Malibu crowd. Ramon was, by comparison, a real loner. He was very shy, very introverted.

"But Ramon was a great dancer! We were in a cabaret-type show, on the same program. I sang. He tap danced. He was really very, very good. Very agile and really seemed to enjoy what he was doing. I remember that his mom and dad were at the performance. They were very proud of him and he seemed pleased to have done well."

English teacher Berkley Blatz also remembered Ramon: "I sponsored a ballroom dancing club and was in charge of the cabaret night each year. Ramon was very much into tap dancing. In the first years, his tap-dancing auditions were very good technically, but he was rather mechanical. Didn't project a lot of zip, charisma. But he was a regular at the dance studio. He worked hard to get his tap dancing perfect. He eventually developed a style with skill. He was so very shy."

Although he neither led the football team to victory nor caused any disciplinary havoc on campus during his high school years, Ramon experienced his own version of rebellion. Emerging from behind a very conservative image, he managed to amaze friends and raise family eyebrows when he became involved in punk music and the punk lifestyle; he even dyed his hair blue.

Ramon's punk pose initially turned off straight-arrow Emilio, but in the end became the basis for his *Repo Man* character study. As a result, the two brothers were brought closer together than ever.

As Emilio remembered it, Ramon didn't just have blue hair—it was a "bunch of colors." And, he recalled, Ramon was "into the leather. I was real down on it for a long time . . . I think I feared the whole movement, because it seemed so dark.

"Then I got this script for *Repo Man*, and the lead character is a punk. So I started listening to the music and going to the clubs, and I began to understand what the punk movement was all about, and understanding where my brother was coming from at that point. So for me it was an important film on a personal level."

"The kids certainly have all raised some hell in their days," said a family friend. "Ramon with his punk period; both Charlie and Emilio with their illegitimate children. But they are a deeply rooted Catholic family, and the entire family is exceptionally close. Even the grandchildren spend a lot of time at the Sheen homestead, where baby pictures are displayed all over the place."

Surrounded by the movie business as he has been all his life, it was inevitable that acting would rub off on Ramon in spite of his early avoidance. In the spring of 1985, Ramon Sheen—by now using his combination of Martin's names in his work—made his first film appearance. He put his tap shoes aside long enough to join his dad in Paris to act in *State of Emergency*, an "issue" movie that was given only a limited release.

Ramon has also worked onstage, appearing in *One Flew Over the Cuckoo's Nest* at the Burt Reynolds Jupiter

Theater, and at The Pasadena Playhouse in a production of the dark comedy, *House of Blue Leaves*. Ramon was cast as Ronnie Shaughnessey alongside costars Buck Henry, Rue McClanahan, and Chloe Webb. (And since Chloe Webb played Nancy in the definitive punk movie, *Sid & Nancy*, the two certainly had a topic of conversation backstage.)

In early 1987, Ramon completed his first costarring role in a major feature film: *Turn Around*, a British-Norwegian production shot on location in Oslo. The film starred Eddie Albert (yet another Hollywood dynasty member) playing a magician who uses his special brand of magic to avenge his son's death.

Today, Ramon feels comfortable slipping into his dad's— and brothers'—shoes as yet another acting Sheen. He admitted, "I really needed to get away and have a chance to be on my own as an actor. I did a good job and I really enjoyed it.

"When you grow up as the son of an 'actor's actor,' which is how they refer to my dad, you have to realize that the first step is to become 'your own actor.' I'll soon be approaching that point. I think, in the past, I never gave myself a chance, and felt that everything had to be accomplished overnight. That's no longer the case. There's time, and I've decided that I deserve that time to develop."

Ramon is again very much his father's son in the area of social awareness. He was eager to appear as narrator and on-camera host for the Group W production of *Street Shadows*, a documentary that dealt with runaways and street kids. Ramon expressed pleasure at being able to bring attention to the plight of the million-and-a-half kids who find themselves without homes each year.

"You know," he said, "it's pretty common for people to believe that when you've been brought up as I have been in a very close-knit family—and, let's face it, in very affluent surroundings—that you have no concept of being jobless, homeless, and out on the streets. But that's not so. There are many kids who leave luxurious surroundings because of what they feel are unbearable conditions at home. I've known some friends who have and it's true, things just go from bad to worse.''

As 1987 rolled into 1988, Ramon found himself on location in Vienna, Austria where he was to undertake his first film role as the star of the action. It was in the Mellon-Skilling production of *Young Werewolves in Love.* Tom Swerdlow, Stacey Nelkin, and Michael J. Pollard costar in the feature, which casts Ramon as Sam, a young computer whiz who ''is a nonbeliever. He doesn't buy all that werewolf stuff,'' Ramon said. ''But he learns, he learns!''

Again in family tradition, Ramon diligently prepared for his work in *Young Werewolves*—and not just on the character. He spent ten weeks studying German prior to leaving for Europe, even though his character was to be pure American. ''I just never go anywhere expecting that everyone is going to speak my language, so I feel it's necessary to get at least some of the basics of their language down. It's really just a matter of courtesy, and it makes me feel a lot more comfortable knowing I don't have to depend on someone else's kindness to help me get along in a foreign country.''

▪ 21 ▪

The Ladies of the House

JANET TEMPLETON ESTEVEZ, THE FIRST AND ENDURING LOVE OF Martin Sheen's life, has remained the strength and substance that unites this unusually cohesive clan. But who is this matriarch, this power behind the throne? Janet does not grant interviews; she does not dispense her rules for raising a happy and successful family to women's magazines. She seeks no limelight for herself, but keeps her brood sane while they stand in theirs. She is the rock; she grounds them all.

"Janet is a very sweet woman, but she's also very strict," said a family friend. "Marty's much more liberal, even in the home; Janet sets the rules. She's the authoritarian and Marty's everyone's buddy. The kids will jabber about their dad. They'll talk comparatively very little about their mother, although her presence is felt in the phrase 'our parents' that pops into conversations. Janet has her own interests—charity projects of her own choosing—but she's basically a homebody. An old-fashioned housewife in the very best sense."

161

Content to stay in the shadows, Janet is revealed most through the comments and observations of those who love her. Her influence on her husband and his respect for her opinions are clear. So is his devotion to her. His feelings have emerged again and again over the years in numerous interviews; they bespeak a wife who is loving, willful ("I'm not nuts about the movies. I go because Janet drags me") and a no-nonsense protector of her loved ones.

Sheen told director Emile de Antonio during a 1982 *American Film* interview that it was Janet who saved his life during the physical and emotional crises of *Apocalypse Now*. He recalled:

"Janet was really the truth during all of this. I was caught between the part I was playing and my responsibility as a father, husband, lover. I had to deal with two different things every day: my day at work and my day at home. Janet became the enemy of the producing company. They didn't like her; she was a radical; she objected to everything. She was the only one—I didn't realize it at the time—who had my whole being at heart.

"She never did let up, never once did give in. She said to them, 'No, you can't see him. I don't give a damn. I don't want you to bother him. Get the hell out of here. I don't give a damn who you are.'

"As long as I live I'll never forget, when I was being wheeled down to the emergency room, that she took my hand and she said: 'It's only a movie, babe.' And then I started getting well. She stood between me and them."

Janet even took care of Marlon Brando on that primitive filming location. He often had supper with the Sheens and appreciated Janet's thoughtfulness. "Janet had gotten grains, oatmeal, and so on, foods that didn't make you sick. She had forty cases of Perrier sent over, and it saved a lot of problems for Marlon. He used to send her flowers every day," Martin proudly boasted to de Antonio.

The woman's care and concern does not stop with friends

and family. While Martin was still recuperating from his heart attack in the Manila hospital, a very poor man was brought in, himself suffering from a heart seizure. Because he had no money, the hospital administration refused to treat him. As Martin recounted several years later, "Janet went crazy. She grabbed her purse and pulled out all her money and shoved it at the nurse and screamed, 'Get this man to intensive care immediately!' He actually took my old room in intensive care."

Even when Janet is not at his elbow, her presence plays a part in Martin's thoughts and actions. While in India working on *Gandhi*, Sheen was often besieged by beggars. A particular incident wrenched his heart: A little one-armed girl actually hung to the bumper of a cab Sheen was in after he had given her a few coins. He remembered thinking, "What would my wife Janet do in this situation?" before putting that child in the cab with him and taking her with him everywhere he went that day.

But Martin and Janet are not just two peas in a pod. She is not even Roman Catholic, as vital as that faith is to Martin's being. And her political activism is limited to bailing her husband out of jail and providing transportation to and from the occasional nuclear testing site. Martin is quick to point out, as he did in an *US* magazine interview in 1986, "Janet and I don't depend on each other for happiness, but we are each other's support.

"We never agreed on anything in our whole lives. We are temperamentally totally unalike. I'm very volatile, a typical Leo. She's an Aries, very bright and sensitive, with a great sense of humor. It's not a case of the lion laying down with the lamb; it's a case of the lion laying down with the ram!"

Elsewhere he has also admitted, "Not until recently did I realize that she's my teacher. She constantly demands growth from me. Janet even got me into yoga, which was an extraordinary thing for me to do. It's been a great source of energy and self-knowledge for me. She leads me into a lot of positive things."

For Emilio, Janet is family center. "We've always been a very close-knit family. My dad taught me to trust myself and to always search for the truth in whatever I was doing. My mother is very strong and pragmatic. She grounded me."

For third-born son Charlie, his mother is the benevolent guardian who sent him off to film *Platoon* in the Philippines with "eight hundred boxes of things" to keep him healthy and happy. Nor is she afraid to give a helping dose of criticism when that's required. When Charlie went on Joan Rivers's *Late Night* talk show, he bragged publicly about his new Porsche, and said that he just about got a speeding ticket on the Pacific Coast Highway.

Like any doting mom, Janet watched the show. "When I got home," remembered Charlie, "I called my mother to see what she thought. And she says, 'You're driving a car that I cosigned for at a hundred-and-thirty miles an hour?!'"

Charlie described his mother to journalist Leonora Langley as "the warden of the family. She doesn't miss a beat. She's cool and only dishes out constructive criticism, deep concern. If she was a maid and dad was a carpenter, I'd still love them to death.

"The stability of our parents' marriage has certainly helped us all as actors," continued Charlie. "Raising a child is a bit like building a skyscraper. It takes two years to build the foundation and six months to construct the building. You have to invest in a firm grounding. If a kid has had that, he has something to fall back on."

It's not unusual to find a family where there are a number of children of one gender . . . and one last one of the other. Normally, the parents kept trying for a boy. In this family, everyone was waiting for Renee.

The baby of the family and the long-hoped-for girl, Renee was particularly precious to her dad. One afternoon when she was about six, Martin was playing with her on the beach and the little girl wandered out of sight. Her father, terrified, was sure she'd gotten pulled into the surf. Even though he can't swim a stroke, he was about to dive into the waves in a panic to look for her, when she shyly reappeared from behind a sand dune.

"I'd die in a minute if it meant saving one of my kids," said Martin. "I knew if I tried to save her, I'd likely die. But I also knew that if I didn't try, I'd die, too."

Like many young girls, Renee developed a love for horses as she grew up. And like many young girls from comfortable families, she was able to indulge her interest. She started taking lessons when she was just seven, and went on to local competitions. "She's a terrific equestrian," said Martin. "She's won several state amateur titles in her class and division."

Charlie said of Renee, "She'll probably turn out to be the talent in the family." But it's not clear if he means as an athlete, actress, or writer. She excels in all three areas. Currently, Charlie and Renee are collaborating in at least one arena. Together, they are penning a book of verse tentatively titled *Poems From the Big White Phone*.

Renee, as it happens, is a great lover of poetry and freeform prose; her favorite writers are Allen Ginsberg and Jack Kerouac. One reporter noted that Renee is more apt to be found browsing in bookstores than carousing at dance clubs. Her dad puffs up with pride about her literary abilities, saying, "She has a real gift for writing, both poetry and prose."

Still, you can hardly be a Sheen kid without taking at least a stab at acting. And Renee, too, is giving it a go. "When I told my parents, they weren't gung-ho about it," she said. "They just told me I'd better realize what I was getting into. I guess because I'm the only girl in the family, I've never been made to feel like I had to do what they were doing."

She managed to snag a small role in the hit action picture *Lethal Weapon*, starring heartthrob Mel Gibson and Danny Glover, which was released by Warner Brothers in early 1987. Unfortunately, her one scene never made it to the big screen; it was cut in the editing. She also played a sociopath from the South End of Boston in the telemovie *The Room Upstairs*. This gave her a chance to work with such well-respected players as Stockard Channing, Sam Waterston, and Linda Hunt.

In the CBS Schoolbreak Special, *Babies Having Babies*, Renee was directed by her father in the role of Maxine, a punkish unwed mom-to-be who is not nearly as streetwise as she likes to pretend. Her character is strong but sensitive. And even when no words are spoken, the expression in her eyes reveals both strength and vulnerability.

Renee looks like a Sheen, resembling Emilio more closely than she does Charlie. But those warm, hooded eyes—almost uncanny in their ability to convey thoughts and feelings—are as marked in her as in all the others. Janet and Renee, the distaff side of the Sheen-Estevez ensemble, show every bit of the strength, compassion, and talent that the more high-profile menfolk exhibit. They are part of the balance that makes the whole, in this case, greater than the sum of its parts.

■ 22 ■

Looking Ahead

"I'VE BEEN LUCKY ENOUGH TO WORK MOST OF MY ADULT LIFE as an actor," said Martin Sheen, "and wouldn't change that for anything in the world. You have success every now and then, but most of the time you have commercial failures. You just have to go along and do the best you can, enjoy the work, and let it go."

As 1988 went into gear, Martin was getting into gear on a film adaptation of the Broadway stage play, *Da*, produced by his company—Smith-Greenblatt Productions—and starring himself. (The firm also produced *Babies Having Babies* and the controversial Berlin project that helped delay Sean Penn's visit to prison.) But moviemaking is only one small part of his plans for the upcoming year: Activism and family pursuits take top priority.

"I don't even think of myself as having a career anymore," he said. "I tried to separate 'career' from 'life' and realized that was all I had: a career. My career was everything, at the expense of my family and my health and my spirituality. Discovering that spelled freedom for me.''

But this doesn't mean that, at forty-eight, Martin Sheen will be retiring from the limelight, or turning into some kind of martyr or saint. ''I still love my cigarettes, my pool, my car, my flesh, my image,'' he said. ''Part of me still loves all that shit. I try to change, but I do it inch by inch. I wish I did more.''

Martin, Charlie, and Emilio were all together on Christmas Eve of 1987, dishing out meals for the homeless at a Los Angeles Skid Row mission. And all three will also appear in a movie together—perhaps with Ramon and Renee, too—if the right script can be found.

In the meantime, Emilio and Charlie will both be seen in the Columbia production *Young Guns*, costarring Lou Diamond Phillips (*La Bamba*) and Keifer Sutherland (son of Donald and costar of *Lost Boys* and *Bright Lights, Big City*).

''The press would have you think that there's a big rivalry between Emilio and me,'' said Charlie, ''but nothing could be further from the truth. We're a very close family. We sit around laughing about all that stuff that's written about us.''

Emilio is researching new script ideas and writing a few, while his next movie—*Ask the Dust*, directed by Daniel Vigne (*The Return of Martin Guerre*)—goes into production. And now Charlie has turned screenwriter as well, with Orion optioning an action tale he penned with writing partner H.L. Hacking.

Charlie is also appearing in the Cinema Group production of *Never on a Tuesday*, in which he'll sport a huge scar across his handsome face and talk in an exaggerated Southern drawl. He has called it ''my most extreme character role to date.''

Charlie has decided to calm down a little bit as the decade draws to a close; he's more likely to be driving around in an old Bonneville than in his Porsche (because it's "safer") and he's traded his beachfront apartment for a black-on-black decorated home in the Malibu hills. He's spending a lot of time deep-sea fishing, a hobby he took up two years ago while vacationing in Hawaii.

"The moments of being alone are getting harder to find," he said, "but they're still there, and always will be."

And it is this aloneness, this time of unity with self—for Charlie, for Emilio, for their father—that produces the unique inner communication that we see on the screen. And hope to see for many years to come.

Filmography

MARTIN SHEEN . . . FILMS

The Incident, 1967
The Subject Was Roses, 1968
Catch-22, 1970
No Drums, No Bugles, 1971
When the Line Goes Through, 1971
A Time to Every Purpose, 1971
The Forests Are Nearly All Gone Now, 1971
Pickup on 101, 1972
Rage, 1974
Badlands, 1974
The Legend of Earl Durand, 1975
The Cassandra Crossing, 1977
The Little Girl Who Lives Down the Lane, 1977
Apocalypse Now, 1979
Final Countdown, 1980
Loophole, 1980

Gandhi, 1982
That Championship Season, 1982
In the King of Prussia, 1982
Enigma, 1983
Man, Woman, and Child, 1983
The Dead Zone, 1983
Eagle's Wing, 1983
Firestarter, 1984
To an Infinite Power, 1984
In the Name of the People, 1984
Chain Reaction, 1985
State of Emergency, 1985
Judgment in Berlin, 1985
The Believers, 1987
Wall Street, 1987
Siesta, 1987
Da, 1988

MARTIN SHEEN . . . TELEVISION MOVIES

Then Came Bronson, 1969
Goodbye, Raggedy Ann, 1971
Mongo's Back in Town, 1971
Welcome Home, Johnny Bristol, 1971
That Certain Summer, 1972 (Emmy nomination withdrawn at Sheen's request)
Pursuit, 1972
Crime Club, 1972
Letters From Three Lovers, 1973
Catholics, 1973
Message to My Daughter, 1973
Harry O, 1973
A Prowler in the Heart, 1973
The Execution of Private Slovik, 1974 (Emmy nomination)
The Story of Pretty Boy Floyd, 1974
The California Kid, 1974

The Missiles of October, 1974
Death of a Salesman, 1975
Romain Gary, 1975
The Last Survivors, 1975
Sweet Hostage, 1975
Taxi!!!, 1978 (Emmy nomination)
Blind Ambition, 1979 (Emmy nomination, withdrawn at Sheen's request)
In the Custody of Strangers, 1982
Kennedy, 1983
No Place to Hide, 1983
Choices of the Heart, 1983
The Guardian, 1984
The Long Road Home, 1980 (Daytime Emmy award)
Out of Darkness, 1985
Consenting Adults, 1985
The Atlanta Child Murders, 1985 (Emmy nomination withdrawn at Sheen's request)
Samaritan, 1986
Babies Having Babies, 1986 (Emmy award, Direction; Emmy nomination, Executive Producer)
My Dissident Mom, 1987

MARTIN SHEEN . . . SELECTED OTHER TELEVISION

East Side, West Side
As the World Turns
Outer Limits
The Defenders
Medical Center
Route 66
Mannix
Matt Lincoln
Cade's County
Naked City
My Three Sons

The Mod Squad
The F.B.I.
Cannon
Hawaii Five-O
Mission: Impossible

EMILIO ESTEVEZ . . . FILMS

Tex, 1982
The Outsiders, 1983
Repo Man, 1984
That Was Then . . . This Is Now, 1985
The Breakfast Club, 1985
St. Elmo's Fire, 1985
Maximum Overdrive, 1985
Wisdom, 1986
Stakeout, 1987
Ask the Dust, 1988
Young Guns, 1988

EMILIO ESTEVEZ . . . TELEVISION

Making the Grade, 1981
To Climb a Mountain, 1981
17 and Going Nowhere, 1982
''Nightmares'' episode of *Amazing Stories*, 1982
In the Custody of Strangers, 1982

CHARLIE SHEEN . . . FILMS

Grizzly II: The Predator, 1984
Red Dawn, 1984
Lucas, 1985
The Wraith, 1986
Ferris Bueller's Day Off, 1986
Boys Next Door, 1986
Platoon, 1986
Three for the Road, 1987

No Man's Land, 1987
Wall Street, 1987
Eight Men Out, 1988
Johnny Utah, 1988
Never on a Tuesday, 1988
Young Guns, 1988

CHARLIE SHEEN . . . TELEVISION

The Execution of Private Slovik, 1974
Amazing Stories, 1982
Silence of the Heart, 1983
Out of Darkness, 1985

RAMON SHEEN . . . FILMS

The Dead Zone, 1983
State of Emergency, 1985
Turn Around, 1987
Young Werewolves in Love, 1988

RAMON SHEEN . . . TELEVISION

The Fourth Wise Man, 1980
Street Shadows, 1987

RENEE ESTEVEZ . . . FILMS

Loophole, 1980
Lethal Weapon, 1987

RENEE ESTEVEZ . . . TELEVISION

The Atlanta Child Murders, 1985
Babies Having Babies, 1986
The Room Upstairs, 1987
Growing Pains, 1987
MacGyver, 1987

ABOUT THE AUTHORS

Los Angeles-based journalist Lee Riley has covered the celebrity scene for the past eight years. Her previous books include *Patrick Duffy* (St. Martin's Press) and *Tom Cruise* (Pinnacle Press). A former disc jockey and professional dancer, she is currently working on a history of Hollywood stuntmen. Ms. Riley devotes her free time to counseling young people about drug and alcohol awareness.

David Shumacher is an investigative reporter who has collaborated in the past on numerous biographies of celebrities, including Rock Hudson, Don Johnson, Robin Williams, and Vanna White. Also known as a photojournalist, Mr. Shumacher will have a calendar of his work released in 1989. Originally from Chicago, he currently lives with his wife, Tamara, in northern California.